CHIEF EXECUTIVE MOM

Run Your Home
Like You Mean
Business

Jennifer Lopez

Editorial Project Management: Karen Rowe, www.karenrowe.com
Cover Design: This Functional Family in collaboration with
Shake Creative, ShakeTampa.com
Inside Layout: Ljiljana Pavkov

Printed in the United States

ISBN: 978-1-7339601-0-6 (paperback)
ISBN: 978-1-7339601-1-3 (ebook)

To Everyday Moms

"The greatest discovery of all time is that a person can change his future by merely changing his attitude."

– *Oprah Winfrey*

Table of Contents

CHIEF EXECUTIVE MOM

Run Your Home
Like You Mean
Business

Foreword
by Micala Quinn

*O*nce upon a time...

Isn't that how books are supposed to begin? Or maybe just the books my daughter keeps asking me to read... we are in a princess phase. So, I will borrow that phrase.

Once upon a time, I was a full-time teacher juggling a virtual assistant side hustle, motherhood, marriage, and all that life entails. *Juggling* might not be the right word. That sounds like I was successfully balancing everything, and I was not. How about *poorly* juggling my motherhood, marriage, and life? Basically, things were getting dropped. A lot.

As someone whose podcast and courses are designed to help stay-at-home/work-from-home Moms jumpstart their freelance career so they can experience freedom, flexibility, and financial stability while raising their families, I know that the content in this *Chief Executive Mom* will have value for you.

As my side hustle morphed into my full-time gig, and then transformed into my group coaching program, I'm sad to say things did not get easier. Owning a business is hard. Owning a business *and* your life — sometimes that seems darn near impossible. But it shouldn't be this way and it doesn't have to be, especially with Jennifer's actionable approach to managing your home.

One thing I learned when I grew my online base to over 20k+ followers in less than two years was that I could not do everything alone. When I heard about Jennifer's work, we both knew that we had a shared mission. Jennifer helps moms free up time by systemizing and delegating, while I teach them how to earn extra income with that free time. Together we are one dynamic duo!

What I love about Jennifer and the work she has put into her career is how clearly it shows the importance of women owning their power in the workplace and the home. It's 2019 — it's time moms should stop feeling like they have to choose between one or the other! We are allowed to be strong, powerful leaders *with a* baby (or babies) on our hips. Jennifer has made it her mission to give the *most* vital gift to women — their time. It's no wonder her business was awarded Best Start Up & Best New Business in its inaugural year.

Unfortunately for the majority of us, Assistant Pro does not service our area *(yet!)*. Fortunately for **all** of us, anyone reading this book can apply Jennifer's tips & tricks today to step off that hamster wheel of never-ending to-dos & start running your household like the boss you have always been.

When you first think about running your home like a CEO, it seems daunting, right? Who wants to run around barking orders at their children or husband?

Well no one, obviously. And the most successful CEOs don't do this, either. And let me just say from experience, husbands don't respond well to this approach either.

As Jennifer demonstrates, the best bosses focus on team *engagement*, not management. We don't expect our colleagues to read your mind, but we sure do have a difficult time communicating when we need help at home to our spouses, right?

Inside this book, you will learn the fundamental mindset switch to **stop** operating as the sole proprietor of your home and start allowing your partner and children to work *with* you — to build a true family unit. We are all in this together. Jennifer walks you through a step-by-step process to inspire and empower your entire family to take pride and ownership in helping **you** at home.

Are you ready to regain time in your schedule? Step into your power as Chief Executive Mom. You will never hold a more important title.

And all the moms lived happily ever after.

Because their kids put away their own laundry. And their partner did the dishes.

The End.

Micala Quinn
Mom of 3
Owner/Founder
The Live Free Podcast

Acknowledgements

I would like to thank my children for training me in the ways of motherhood. Every day we have together is a day we learn together and I am grateful for all four of you and each of your special gifts. Vanessa, for your conviction; Jacob, for your compassion; Lucy, for your courage, and Nora, for your curiosity.

Thank you to my friends and colleagues in the business world that held my hand as I re-entered adult society to follow my dreams. Thank you to my accountability coaches and partners with special thanks to Jodi McLean and Jeanine McCleod for being key motivators throughout the writing process.

Thank you to my editor, Karen Rowe for taking a bunch of my words and turning them into my story.

And thank you to my biggest fan and best friend: my husband, Mark. I don't know that I'll ever have the words to express how much I appreciate you and your fierce support for my gigantic dreams. I love every lifetime with you.

1:

Welcome to Your New Role

Wife. Mom. CFO. Executive chef. Maintenance director. Event coordinator. Nurse. Psychologist. Sheriff. Scheduling manager. Landscape architect. Interior designer. Superintendent. Physical trainer. Nutritionist. Wife. Mom.

If you asked me when I was 17 what I wanted to be when I grew up, the answer was very simple: a stay-at-home mom. I was in college at the time getting an education that I thought would lead to a few years as a teacher, so I could still have summers off. But after that, all I wanted was a school bus full of kids that I birthed and raised would call me Mom. It was the only thing I wanted. Most people would raise an eyebrow at my answer because I had "so much potential," why wouldn't I want a "real" career? It was clear to me these people failed to see homemaking for what it is: a full-time, multi-faceted career in and of itself.

At that same ripe age of 17, I met a boy. We dated for a few years before I decided to hastily get a jump on my dream job. We bought a house, got married three weeks later and three months after that I was pregnant with my first daughter, Vanessa. I had just about eight months to prepare and get the house in order before the main event. I read the books, decorated the nursery, attended birthing class and before I knew it, Vanessa was here.

Twenty-six months later another little one, my son Jacob, arrived. It wasn't long, however, before I knew I had committed to a marriage that would outgrow itself. We both quickly—and happily—moved on to new marriages. Now, in the right union with a wonderful man named Mark, my second and third daughters, Lucy and Nora, came very quickly to complete our family of four.

Our family was mostly harmonious but after the honeymoon phase, I felt stress creep in. I was determined to fight it, but I couldn't exactly put my finger on what was causing the stress until months later when I had a realization: it was my routine that was killing us.

That's right, *my routine*.

Just like dinner, everyone in my house preferred something different and I was so obsessed with my own plan that I stupidly—and unknowingly—was completely ignoring everyone else's work flow.

That's when the research really began. I became an avid researcher of my family, noting my children and husband's patterns, habits, and personalities. Doing so made me feel like I was observing behavior in the wild at times (but don't tell them that!) Really, it didn't matter how excited I was about the plans, what mattered was how excited *they* were about the plans, because they had to buy-into and own them too. They had to stay clean and educated, they had to be contributing members of our household. It dawned on me that being a homemaker is not about keeping a household in check, it's about making the members of the habitat feel like they belong and that they are an important part of something. It's about making a team out of my family—and it was up to me as the CEO of the household to build that team.

Consider how you feel when you're in the right work environment. You enjoy the people, you feel connected, you are productive, and you grow personally and professionally. Just as a CEO has everything to do with a work culture and building a team that allows you to feel this way, so does the homemaker have everything to do with setting the tone in the home. As a homemaker, you are the CEO of your household—the visionary who establishes the culture. How do you feel about your role as homemaker now? Are your behaviors reflective of a homemaker who is really the CEO of the household?

Your Household, Inc.

I want you to know that I've been there. After nearly a decade in general management in retail and having given birth to Lucy, my husband and I decided our best course of action was for me to stay home full time and invest in our children and family life. I was incredibly grateful for the opportunity.

Those years saw me at home working my butt off every day, some days more than others. Some days I felt discouraged. Most days I felt discouraged, in fact, because even my best days sometimes went unnoticed and unappreciated. My house looked great when it looked great, my kids worked really hard when they worked hard. My husband really loved me when he loved me.

But inside, something was still nagging at me. I thought that because I got married and had kids in my early twenties that the best thing I could do with my life was educate my kids and make them the best people this world has ever seen.

Even though I left collecting a paycheck behind, I never really left management. It wasn't long before I was running my household the same way I ran my stores: strategically and efficiently.

I had a profit and loss statement, a daily checklist, a communications and scheduling binder. I even forced my husband into a weekly check-in and recap!

While I was doing all that—with no family support—I must have wished a thousand times that I had a personal assistant. Not *all* the time. Just during the moments when I felt most exhausted, like when the baby stayed up all night, or when we were throwing the kids' birthday parties, or on a Sunday night after a vacation when we had *all that laundry*. I just wanted a little break every now and then. And I knew I wasn't the only mom that felt this way.

I decided to turn my homemaking and managerial skills into a business offering and founded Assistant Pro, a company dedicated to helping middle-class busy families get their time back. We specialize in helping middle-class busy families with every dayeveryday repetitive tasks. The aim of the company is to afford-ably give you as homemakers the break they deserve.

When it comes down to it, I do what I do because I've been where you are: motivated, productive, over-whelmed and defeated. I do what I do because while you *can* do it all, you shouldn't *have to*. We want to help you systematize your task lists and free up your time so you can keep doing what you're doing, making your own magic in the world.

When I was a stay-at-home mom, I ran my home efficiently; but running the home is a 24-hour-a-day job. Even with my family on board as team of help-ers and doers, I still wished for a little relief from the never-ending chores. When I envisioned Assistant Pro, it was really just one mother's dream for her family to have a little guilt-free break without the house falling apart. It was the extra hand I would'vewould have loved to have had as needed.

Now that vision has become my reality: Assistant Pro is a competent, affordable helper to take some stress off your plate. You should be able to have your moments to yourself, in a peaceful space. You should be the most productive version of you and not have to worry about the tedious, everyday tasks that will always require your attention: both on the home front (laundry, dishes, and meals on) and at the home front or office (scheduling, taking care of calls, and sending gratitude notes at the office.)

Creating Assistant Pro has given me an opportunity to refine my systems in a way that I can now teach and share with my clients. It was clear from the moment I first opened the doors to Assistant Pro that my clients shared the feeling of overwhelm and a sense of lack of time and energy. As I sought to create a system that would allow my clients to free up their time, give them more energy and feel more confident, I came up with a 3-step Methodology that speaks directly to the heart of the matter. These three steps are decisiveness, insightfulness, and consistency. While I discuss these steps in-depth in Chapters 8 through 10, you'll find each concept is applicable throughout the book. You can check out the methodology in Appendix A.

The chapters ahead pinpoint specific areas of the household that can be modified in practice in order to make your household run more efficiently. By appealing to different styles of work flow, you, the homemaker, will work less at making everyone in your household bend to your plan and, instead, assist your family with understanding what motivates them to get stuff done. By implementing the different techniques I share throughout the book, and adopting the Assistant Pro 3-step methodology, you will feel the members of your household buying into their roles as part of the team.

You'll see how your role as homemaker can become that of team-builder, and when that happens, you will have a home that runs smoothly, and a happy, balanced family who feel a keen sense of belonging.

What is the benefit of all of this? Happiness.

With that in mind, I now invite you to retire your current mindset that keeps you trapped feeling like an unappreciated, unpaid, frustrated housewife and step into your new role: Chief Executive Mom.

2:

Get Out of Overwhelm

*H*ere is the problem as I see it: For as long as you can remember, you have wanted to be a wife, a mother, and an overall happy human being. You realize that every day you have this vision of how it all will go.

Then you wake up one morning and wonder what happened. You cook and clean and try not to yell. The stress of it all is aging you. You think back to the time when your dream was all of this and wonder why your reality is not this at all.

Why don't I have enough energy? Why won't anyone in this house cooperate? No matter what I do, it feels like it's never good enough. I've tried to make my house a cozy home. Did I pick the right photo to hang? Put it in the right spot? I've organized the kitchen in the most sensible way, so why aren't the clean dishes and utensils put away in the right spot? I'm tired. No—I'm *exhausted.* The kind of exhaustion that doesn't go away after a good night's. I argue with my kids and my husband. I'm angry with myself for not being better. I could be a better cook. I could keep the house cleaner. I could be nicer, happier, not so reactive. I mean, they're just kids being kids. I'm surrounded by people all the time, but I feel so alone. The weight of all of this is giving me more anxiety. I just wish for some cooperation. What is so hard about putting your clothes away and making your bed? Why am I the only one that puts a decent meal on the table? When does the to-do list end? And if I take a day off—or even just an hour off—how does everything pile up so quickly? It's so discouraging.

I've been there, sister. I've walked a mile in your shoes and I know your pain. I know what it's like to look forward to your significant other coming home and he doesn't notice anything that's been done. He doesn't know what you've taught the kids. He doesn't acknowledge how long it took to prepare the incredible dinner you place in front of him. And it shouldn't matter.

But deep down inside you want to be a good wife to him because he's a good provider for you and you want to show him your love. You want to go the extra mile, but even just doing the bare minimum is bogging you down. Why can't he see? Why can't he see any of this?

I'll tell you why: because he's not a part of it. None of them are. Not the kids, not him, just you. I'm here to wake you up and shake it up. What you are doing isn't working. Sure, maybe you've got it together—sometimes. But that's not the solution. You're just throwing a band-aid on a boo-boo that really needs stitches.

You need to own this. Own that you are doing it wrong. Because if it was right, you wouldn't be feeling this way. Knowing it's wrong will allow you to be open to changing it. And it is time to change.

I know this story. I know it first-hand. I was in a marriage that wasn't so good. I left it. Now I'm in a marriage that I love. It's still hard. But when it's the hardest, it's because of me. It's because I've learned that my light shines brightest when I'm happy. When I am unhappy, my light dims, and my family relationships suffer.

When I'm not happy, however, I've learned to change things so that I allow myself to be happy, and sometimes that rocks the boat. There is a period of discomfort for everyone when this happens. But what I've come to realize is I'm the only one that cares and pays attention to everyone else's discomfort. No kid ever says, "Mom's having a hard time adjusting to my teenage attitude, I better suppress it." My husband doesn't think, "My wife will be unhappy if I don't put the toothpaste away after I use it." I'm the only one worried about it. And I'm teaching my kids that it's okay to be walked on. I'm not upholding my marriage as one between equal partners if I'm putting my spouse's happiness above my own.

Break the Cycle

The longer you struggle alone, trying to please everyone but yourself, and not allowing your family to form as a team around you and the home, the harder it is to break that cycle.

Well guess what? Now is the time to break that cycle. You're reading this book because you know there is more to life than this. You can consistently have those happy moments that you dreamt of when you wished for all of this. The good you do is not just through raising your children. There is still time for you. Yes, there is. We are going to create time for you and still get everything done. So wake up! Wash your face. Put on the clothes that you *want* to wear. I don't care if it's an evening gown. Put it on and feel good. This is important. Put this book down, take a shower, do your hair, throw on some mascara, wear your nice shoes—yes, those impractical ones that you really want to wear. Do that and come back in 90 minutes—it's time to get to work.

3.

Mom First

We all know how the story begins: when you're pregnant it's all about you. People want to touch your belly, everyone asks when you're due, your husband obligingly runs to the store at 11 p.m. to get ice cream when you're craving it. But the moment that little baby makes her grand entrance, *you* fade into the background and everyone's attention and efforts shift to your new addition. It's natural, and there is absolutely nothing wrong with that, because your job now is to keep that little one alive and nurture them.

What we don't realize is that it naturally becomes our habit to put others before ourselves because that's what we practice most in the first two years of a new child being born. And if your pregnancy patterns are anything like mine, that could go on for 8-10 years. What we tend to forget though, is what makes us the special person we are—and in forgetting this specialness, we forget how to nurture and best take care of this special person. Naturally we morph into becoming someone's mom because that is the most important thing we're doing.

But what about you? What else are you? Who else are you? Because you *are* more than your job or duties. What we want to do is reconnect with what makes you so uniquely *you*. Because while being a mom is a wonderful chapter in your life, it is not the only chapter.

Recently I went through an exercise with a group of ladies wherein I asked them who they are and what makes them tick. The first woman to answer introduced herself as "Ryan's mom." I know that seemed like a special answer to her because she cherishes her child and she's proud of raising such a great human being. You can imagine her surprise when I replied, "Yes, but I want to know about *you*."

She froze and then became emotional. She hadn't thought about herself in so long that she couldn't confidently speak to her own characteristics, her own likes and dislikes. I hugged her, because I had been there once too. I let her and the group know that what she was feeling right in that moment was normal.

All of us moms tend to respond that same way at one time or another; "I'm Ashley's mom" or "I'm Jordyn's mom." The truth is there is much more to you, it's just that you may have forgotten what that is. Now it's time to reconnect—because in the reconnecting, you will find new inspiration to be the best you can be, and care for yourself in the best way you can without feeling selfish about it.

Keep in mind, you don't necessarily have to *find* yourself, you just have to *remember* yourself. The best way to do this is to remember and reconnect with what it is that makes you happy. Be patient with yourself as you begin this work. You probably haven't had much time to think because you've been busy keeping your family happy and healthy. It's going to take some time to remember what your passion and life's mission are— and to reconnect with why it's so important to practice exemplary self-care if you are going to run your household like the Chief Executive Mom you are.

When someone asks you if you're making time to take care of yourself, they don't mean are you getting to the grocery store by yourself. The real question is, do you have enough time to self-reflect and remember what drives you every single day? Do you offer the same level of love, support, nurturance and care to yourself as you do to your partner and kids?

I know it's your kids that motivate you every day. I know you wake up because you have to take care of them. You enjoy taking care of them. You love being a mom and you love being homemaker. But there's so much more to you and it's important not to let that go.

This chapter will take you through a few of my top tips for reconnecting with yourself, setting goals and developing a plan that keeps you on track with your goals. It will also help you to then deal with the change that is inevitable as you journey back to being *you*. Feel free to pause and do the exercises in the moment, or bookmark the page and come back to it.

Most of all, take a breath. You're coming back to yourself—thank yourself for having the courage to do this. Taking time to remember yourself is your first step toward taking care of that beautiful creature in the mirror.

Let's start by finding out what makes you happy!

100 Things That Make You Happy

The first exercise is to grab a pen and paper and make a list of 100 things that make you happy.

Since the moment your child was born, life has been a whirlwind series of events revolving around, basically, around keeping everybody alive. When was the last time you thought about what makes *you* happy? Make a list right now of those 100 things—and no less than 100. It has to be that many because you have to take that time to look deeper than what's on the surface. The first few things on your list will be the obvious: kids, husband, pets, parent, clean house, no laundry, floors mopped, watered garden, pictures in the frames, hot meal, and so on. But what lies beyond these?

In my case, it took looking back at things listed that I realized how little I knew myself. Many of the things on my list were not in any way related to my happiness. They were things on my to-do list! I challenge you to find 100 things that truly make you smile.

Here are a few questions to help you generate some ideas:

- What is your favorite food?
- What is your favorite outfit?
- Favorite hair style?
- Favorite song?

If any of these favorites make you smile, what's holding you back from having them right now, all at once? If the excuse is reading this book, put it down and go make yourself happy. Your happiness and self-care come before everything else. I write it here and invite you to say it out loud right now with me: *Self-care is not selfish!* You are your family's Chief Executive Mom: the visionary, the leader. It is time to stop running in place and put your best foot forward. You cannot do that if you are also the disgruntled employee. It's time to get happy. Now, go finish that list!

Connect To Your Purpose

As I mentioned earlier, I myself have four children. My oldest, Vanessa, proved very early on that she was gifted with intelligence. My husband and I discussed time and time again that Vanessa may have the opportunity to be one of those prodigy kids, you know the one that goes to MIT at 12 years old. We pushed and pushed because I thought my job was to change the world through my children.

After a few years of pushing not only Vanessa but all of my children to their limits, I had my moment. I looked in the mirror and didn't recognize what I'd become. I looked older, my hair was undone, I was in yoga pants with the remnants of my toddler's lunch on them, a scene I had grown accustomed to. It was in that moment I realized my mission wasn't to change the world through my children. I still had time—and I didn't want to waste any more of it. I wanted to inspire my kids to do something great because I had done something great myself.

I sat down and made my list of 100 things that make me happy. After doing so, I realized my mission: I want to help other women, — moms in particular moms— who know life the way I know itdidn't recognize what they had become, to realize their full potential, and to not let every dayeveryday chores get in the way of becoming their true selves. I realized I wanted to get involved in my community, I wanted to be involved in non-profit organizations, and I wanted to teach. I didn't know what I wanted to teach but I knew teaching had always been a passion of mine, and that being part of contributing to someone's growth made me happy.

I wrote all my options down on a piece of lined paper. Maybe I would tutor, maybe I would volunteer, or maybe I would just offer my time in a way that helped others reclaim their time.

Now that I had found my purpose and reconnected with myself it was just a matter of laying out the steps to fulfill that promise. Every day I woke up and mapped out my goals. My goals were informed by my top priorities:

how to be a better wife, how to be a better mom, and how to be a better me. Sometimes those three things were in a different order, in fact, *most* days they were in a different order, and that was okay.

The act of connecting with my purpose, myself, and starting to set goals to move me forward really was my version of putting my "oxygen mask" on first. Just like they tell you on a plane to first put on your own oxygen mask before anyone else's, you won't be able to save anyone else around you if you can't save yourself.

This is what I am inviting you to do: reconnect with yourself. Save yourself first. You deserve to wake up in the morning feeling excited about the day you. If you want to be a good, strong leader and you want to carry out your vision for your family, you have to lead by example and take care of the person that's running it all: you!

Setting goals is another step in the process that I personally found effective when it came to fulfilling my purpose. Give yourself goals. Lay out short-term, intermediate, and long-term goals that align with your vision. Make sure each goal moves you forward towards your long-term goals. If they don't, change them.

Make yourself a personal mission statement and then fulfill it. Live by it and speak it out loud to as many people as you can. This is your brand—and your brand is important for you and your family. Above all, you are the leader. You are the CEO. If you don't have a vision for where your company is going, you will not feel the success when you get there.

Of course, your goal sheet will look different than mine because our missions and passions are different. Once you figure out what it is that drives you every single day-the passion that wakes you up before the sun—then this becomes your long-term goal. You can then create a map to reach it by setting small goals on a daily basis.

Plan Your Day

The simplest way to start working with setting goals is to make a plan. Then, write your goals down—not just once, but daily. Write your vision down every day, read it every day, and act on it every day by setting small, achievable goals that always move you forward. Having your vision in front of you will cultivate your passion, keep you mentally organized and on track.

When you're planning your day, pay attention to the tasks that will help you work toward your goals. If being a master chef is your goal, block out time to research new recipes. If becoming an expert on blog writing is part of your long-term goal, then reading, researching, and bidding on work is a good use of time to put on your daily list. If health is a part of your long-term goal, then scheduling exercise time is a good way to use your time. If being an artist is in your plan for happiness, scheduling time to go to the art store to buy your paint is a productive way to spend your day.

Making a plan is important. This is how you'll measure your success as you travel through your vision and goal map on a daily basis. A plan is just like a naviga-tion route on a map. Use your plan to keep yourself on track. If you catch yourself going the wrong way or in the opposite direction, you can always find your way back if you have a definitive place that you're headed.

So let's devise a plan. Do you already have something in place for the family, kids, house, your happiness? The first thing we need to do is evaluate your daily routine:

- What time do you wake up?
- What time do you have to go to work?
- What time do the kids have to get to school?
- What is step one?

Look at how you currently run your days and then check in with your vision. What do you *want* your day to look like? Before we map the vision, let's work on your schedule to be sure all your obligations are fulfilled.

You have a routine whether you realize it or not. Itemize the order in which you take on your day. Dive deep into this. Here's an example of my daily routine, to give you an idea of what I mean.

Jennifer's Daily Routine

- 6:00 a.m.: (I know what you're thinking …no way! But trust me on this one- it doesn't matter what time you actually start your day, just jot it down.)
- 6:00 a.m.: Up and at 'em! Count from five down to one and at one jump out of bed and stand up. Do two sun salutations with deep breathing to get the blood flowing.

- 6:05 a.m.: Shower, wash face, brush teeth, all while listening to a personal development audio book.
- 6:25 a.m.: Get going! Hair, make-up, clothes on. (Still listening to that book!)
- 7:00 a.m.: (on work days) Coffee , smoothie & out the door.
- 7:00 a.m. (on Saturdays) Coffee & to-do list/ schedule.
- 7:00 a.m.: (on Sundays) Coffee & breakfast in bed.
- 8:00 a.m.: Start day with intentions; review daily plan, scheduled tasks, to-do lists, etc. Use a pen and paper or a checklist app and write your checklist down. Plan it out over 30-60 minute increments, assigning each task a timeframe.
- 8:15 a.m.: Get started! From 8:15 a.m. to 3-5 p.m. is the timeframe I use to get things done.
- 5 p.m. to 8 p.m.: Strict family time, usually kid-planned and executed.
- 8-9 p.m.: Start the kids' evening ritual. (If your kids are young, this might look like giving them a bath and reading bedtime stories.) My kids are older now so I use this time to rotate spending a little extra time with them and wrapping up minor chores.
- 9 p.m.: Time to take care of me! Relaxation, skin care, reading/ writing, watching movies, anything that will help me unwind and de-stress.
- 10:00 to 11:00 p.m. is lights out! No matter how structured my day is, if I don't get an ample amount of sleep my mood and productivity are negatively affected the next day. Even if I'm wrapped up in a great Rom-com I pause, sleep, and continue it the

next day as a routine. There will obviously be nights that we go out or stay up a little later, but for the normal routine, I definitely respect that my body needs 6-8 hours of sleep to recharge.

Now create your own schedule, being as detailed as you can. Drawing attention to your daily routine is helpful even if you are not a planner, because it shows you how you are moving through your life. By doing this exercise, you are smoothing the way to start planning and making it less intimidating as you begin.

You might find making little notes with check boxes on the things that you do frequently, like brushing your teeth, eating breakfast, having your cup of coffee, becomes a helpful activity and brings out the planner in you. If that's the case, then it's just about addressing a few more details to put you on the right path for the day. For the remainder of your non-routine—but equally important—tasks, write them down, assign a number to them in terms of priority, and then set a deadline. Space these tasks out appropriately to set yourself up for success!

Of course, I know we are all unique! There are people like me that live and die by checklists and people who don't. What I've learned from working with many different types of people is that there are many people for whom checklists don't work at all. In some cases, this could be because of the risk for failure. For example, my husband feels that if he doesn't tick all the boxes on his to-do list, he is automatically letting himself down. For Mark, seeing unchecked boxes is admitting defeat.

I love checklists because my head is so full of all the things on my to-do list that it brings me ease to write them down one line at a time. By doing this, I no longer have to put pressure on myself to remember those things. I'm comfortable with admitting that I will fail and forget unless I write them down. Therefore, for me this process is a relief because I am being proactive against my failures, which sets me up for success.

Those little checklist boxes aren't about success or failure, however; they are about taking the pressure off yourself so you don't feel like you have a million details swarming in your head like buzzing bees. When our heads are clear, we can live in the moment and be present. We can fill our thoughts with memories, smiles, happy images, daydreaming about our beautiful futures rather than living in a swirl of "to-dos."

Whether you are naturally a planner or not, if you aren't in the habit of doing it already, consider keeping your schedule active in your sight each day and checking items off your to-do lists. This is a useful habit to at least try to establish because the act of looking at the list and ticking off an item reminds us to live on purpose. And when you live on purpose, you live with purpose. Purpose makes you feel fulfilled—and fulfillment is happiness.

Working with a to-do list, we also give ourselves the opportunity to plan effectively—and according to our capacity—and to determine how to delegate and how to outsource. Best of all, if we "fail" today we can still set ourselves up to succeed tomorrow because we're learning from our experience.

Keep in mind, if there is something on your to-do list that you didn't get to, it isn't necessarily because you failed, it's much more likely that the item was not high enough on the priority list. If you find this happening over and over again, take a closer look at the task. Is it something you actually have to do or is there a more enjoyable way to accomplish the task? Is there someone you can outsource it to? At the end of the day, you don't want to get caught in a thought process where you think you are constantly failing yourself because that will send you into an emotional slump. You don't have time for that and you are better than that.

However you approach it, planning, setting goals, and taking stock of how you run your days are all tools to help you connect with yourself. They are ways of showing you in real-time just how aligned you are with your purpose and mission, and whether you're moving forward. There are as many different ways to use these tools as there are unique individuals, so take these ideas and make them your own as you begin to implement them.

Get The Family On Board

My hope for you is that all of these ideas get your gears turning on how you're going to run *Your Household, Inc.* I call it a business because it *is* one. You have the power to be so efficient and supportive that your salary is generated by the money you saved by being a savvy, creative homemaker. This is one of the superpowers of Chief Executive Mom.

That said, be prepared. Change is against human nature. You are about to make a big change by putting yourself first and reconnecting with who you are and what makes you happy. Following the vision towards your purpose is like throwing a pebble into a calm lake. There will be ripples. The little humans that surround you will be affected by this change. Your partner will also be thrown off their game. If your family is not already accustomed to change it could definitely be a source of the frustration happening within the household already.

When I first met my husband, I had lived in the same town, and on the same block, my whole life. After meeting him we moved three times in a matter of six years, which stressed me out greatly. My husband, however, could navigate this much more easily. He lost his mom at a very young age and learned early on that we have to appreciate each moment. Understand no matter what, whether good or bad, each moment eventually passes. This is change.

From the time our children were young we've instilled this in them, inviting them to appreciate the great times they're having and accept their frustrating and sad times in order to understand that every moment has this one thing in common: all of them will pass.

Another important lesson my dear husband taught me very early on as that you can't have the sweet without the sour. There's no such thing as hot without cold and good days feel great when your sad days feel the saddest. Appreciating all of your moments and how the bad reinforces the good is something we all have to accept. If you want your family to accept you moving towards your vision, you have to accept them in their authenticity as well.

You also have to be OK with changing right now. The unknown can be scary but what's scarier than living in the same stagnant comfort zone over and over again for eternity? Get out of the funk and embrace change.

What Change Looks Like

When I first decided I was going to undergo this transformation, one of the decisions I made was to be responsible *to* my children, and not *for* them. I explained to my husband that this meant I was going to stop controlling them and let them live out the consequences of their choices. He said he was one hundred percent on board with that idea.

Saying this and putting it into practice, however, are two different things. The first time I tried, it was after a nice day at the beach. We watched the sun go down on the shoreline before walking across the street to the showers like we always did. This time, instead of me rushing the kids, washing them up and coaching them through, I just stood back and supervised. I didn't say a word.

Jacob was done first, washed, dried, and changed. Nora, only two at the time, was also cleaned and ready in her car seat. Lucy scrubbed herself clean, but then took her time drying. She'd look at me, then dry some more, then look at me again, expecting me to rush her. She changed into dry clothes, smiled at me and went to the car.

Vanessa showered for longer and didn't make eye contact with me. Either she was attempting to push me or she was really, really just enjoying getting cleaned up. Regardless, she kept up the shenanigans for twenty more minutes. I didn't say a word or make a "mom face." It took all I had, but I remained totally patient.

After what seemed like a long time, Vanessa finished. When we got back into the minivan, my husband instantly questioned me.

"Why did that take so long?" Mark said, pulling out of the parking lot.

"I don't know," I answered sweetly. "You'll have to ask Vanessa—I was waiting on her."

My response set him off. He didn't ask Vanessa about it but pressed me. I explained: Vanessa is learning that she is responsible for herself. I am committed to being responsible *to* her, not for her. I reiterated my statement before, and suggested he ask Vanessa.

His angry, final words for the duration of the hour-long car ride were: "How long are you going to keep this up? This is ridiculous."

That evening, I introduced him to the new me and never looked back. I knew that if I reverted after that moment, I risked hurting our marriage. That turning point was a growing pain and we had to get straight through it as fast as we could.

We did get through it, however, and because of this— and several other interactions supporting the same process—we all have better relationships with one another. I am no longer held accountable by Mark for our children. It makes us a part of the same team again. As we grew closer as a team, we noticed our kids got along better because they noticed the team dynamic and mimicked it.

This simple willingness to change on my part shifted so much in the family. It was no longer us versus them, parents versus kids. There was no more, "Dad said..." It was no longer a hierarchy in which we had to answer on behalf of one another. Instead, everyone was encouraged to represent only themselves.

This was the start of a new way of being, one which eventually included Mark and I showing the kids what it means not to blame one another, to talk it out and direct one's attention to the problem directly instead of in a passive way. Mark, especially, taught the kids to be confrontational in a positive way.

Before that day at the beach, Mark only expected me to "parent the kids." He had to overcome a lot to look our adorable children in the eyes and question their decision-making. However, by being willing to do that, he stopped being judgmental of their decision-making. In fact, he started reconnecting with the kids in a loving way we hadn't seen since they were babies.

The more one parent assumes the role of caretaker, the more the other actually disconnects. When you're only there for the love and hugs, you miss out on the real personalities that are being developed under your roof.

I always played bad cop as a way of helping to keep the kids' relationship with Mark positive, but in doing so I was keeping them from knowing one another on a deeper level.

My willingness to put myself first, investigate my happiness and make it a relentless pursuit, along with jumping into change and deciding deliberately to back off when it came to the kids and their decisions, has led my family to becoming much better at interacting with each other on all levels.

Someone told me recently that in all his years, he has never made a bad decision, because if he knew it was bad he wouldn't have done it. What you did yesterday, a month ago, a year ago was the best choice you could've made in that moment. But today is the day to make a different choice. One that will bring discomfort to your whole family and one that will bring discomfort to you. It's not easy to wake up and stand up for yourself out of nowhere, but it's your responsibility to do so. It's your responsibility to lead by example, motivate your team, bring clarity to the vision, and love everyone uncondi- tionally, even (and especially) yourself.

Know That You Are Valuable

I know this chapter has been meaty and possibly tree-shaking for you. But stick with it—you deserve this. If you haven't done so already, take the time today to write down your age and your meaning of life. What is the mean- ing of life? It's simple: The meaning of your life is made up of the words you choose to define you. Start with writing out a list of ten adjectives you would like to practice. Examples: Hardworking, Athletic, Musical, Funny, Understanding, Caring, Helpful, Happy, Loveable, Sympathetic.

Write down your list of words to use as you move through each day that remind you how you want to be perceived. Re-introduce yourself to the world living by the guidelines and the standard to which you hold yourself. Keep that paper in your planner. Set your alarm daily and speak your words out loud. Be that person every day. When you are faced with a choice or an obstacle, use your words to define your response or reaction.

As a parent, there are so many components that we have to hold together. It makes you wonder exactly what consumed your thoughts before you were a mother. Pre-parenting, you thought you understood what true exhaustion was. Post-baby, you might look back and laugh at your younger self for what you would have called chronic fatigue.

Because being a mother is all-consuming at times, this is the inherent danger of our job. We are constantly under threat of losing ourselves, to our children, to our partners, to life itself. Worse, so many mothers fail to value themselves, or their contributions to the home. I know, I've been there.

Homemaking is often perceived as an undervalued role in society, and mothers bear the emotional brunt of this more than anyone else. How many mothers do you know lacking confidence, or failing to truly value the work they do in the home?

It's time for this to change. If you're afraid to share your gifts and live fully in your sense of self-worth and value, it's time to figure out a way to move beyond that. It is okay to be confident and embrace your gifts in a way that is not boastful.

Stand up and say it:

- I am a good mom.
- I am a good wife.
- I am the best, most qualified and capable person to be running my household.
- I am the Chief Executive Mom of my home and I run the household like I mean business.

4:

Team-Building

Just as a successful company is run by a strong CEO, one who understands the value of empowering work cultures and building teams, so is a household stronger when the person in charge—in this case, YOU—empowers and builds her team (your partner and kids).

Think of your household for a moment, and where you have challenges. Let me guess: it's hard to get the kids to do chores, right?

Upkeep of the house is likely your biggest problem. I can tell you firsthand that taking on chores first as a strategy to changing the household dynamic is like brushing your teeth while chewing Oreos—a complete waste of time.

You feel that chores are your biggest challenge when, in fact, teamwork is actually your biggest challenge. Not just with your husband, but with your children too. If you are thinking that your children are too small to be involved or to be a team players, you are wrong. I'm sorry to be so harsh, but it's true. Read any quality book on leadership, whether in the business world or leadership in general, and you'll find that the most effective leaders are the ones that build strong teams and empower those individuals within that team. In the case of Team Your Household, nobody should be on the bench.

When I came to this realization, I felt horrible that I had excluded my team for so long. I had been benching my players without even giving them an opportunity to bat!

After I had this insight, I changed things in the household. As a result, all of my four children received their first "chore" (even at two years old or younger.) Of course, I received pushback whenever I explained this to my friends and family, but I'll challenge you with this: Think about any job you've ever worked or every team you have ever been a part of, how did you feel when you weren't involved in their success? How did you feel when you were? By not giving every single member of your household a job for which they are held accountable, you are actually making them feel like they are not part of the success of the home, even your smallest member. Now, I'm not suggesting you have your two-year-old mopping the floors or vacuuming. But putting away the shoes? Yes. Putting their cups in the dishwasher or putting them away after they are cleaned? Yes.

It may seem like more of a headache than a help at first, and you have to spend time training your children how to actually do the tasks, but I promise you that you had an employer once who felt the same way about you during training. They had to take time out of their busy schedule, time they'd otherwise have spent doing the thing that makes them profitable, and they had to invest that time training you so you could be the best you could be at that task. Why? So they don't have to worry about that task anymore and the company can move smoothly and efficiently, and ultimately be successful. And for many of us, achieving success means happiness.

Take The Players Off The Bench

As you try to get this process started, you may notice the following:

1. Your children probably give you a lot of trouble when it is time to take care of their chores.
2. Your husband may not do it your way and so now you would rather do it yourself.

Where has that gotten you so far?

Albert Einstein said, "The definition of insanity is doing the same thing over and over again and expecting a different result." Well, my friend, that's what got us to this moment. Are you afraid to relinquish control? Or that by letting the team step up, the floors won't be mopped with the right cleaner? If so, repeat after me: I am controlling. Say it one more time "I am controlling." You've been the boss of the house in a hierarchical way for a long time, and it might feel natural to be controlling. Delegation rarely comes easily, but it is essential, not just for your family, but for *you*. Wouldn't you rather coordinate, train, and delegate than do it all yourself? Or yell at your kids in frustration? This is your chance to stop the insanity. Just know that this growth period of your personal self and the household will be a little bumpy.

If you were thrown into a job with little to no training, accountability or reward, I promise you would be disgruntled too. So let's start with that.

Child Resistance

The real underlying issue with child resistance is the same as with any other grown human being: a person will resist when they feel their opinion doesn't matter or isn't being taken into consideration. A person will resist when they don't feel respected; a person will resist when they feel as though they're being talked down to or talked at or when there is a lack of consideration.

We tend to treat children differently, as if we have this power over them and we're supposed to control and make decisions for them because we know best. While in some cases our experience will help us see clearly and guide them, it's important for us to listen to the voice of our child because "child" just means that they're a smaller person. It does not give us control over them.

When I talk about resistance I'm really talking about not having the type of respect our children have in mind. Too often it's the case that we ourselves can recall getting along with our own parents as very small children and how the brunt of our issues stemmed from when we felt we had the capacity to make decisions for ourselves but our parents still made decisions for us.

There is no numerical age at which time humans are magically granted the ability to make their own choices. This has to do with education, maturity, development, and experience. In that regard every single human being develops at a different pace. It's imperative that we don't attach a number to it. By training your children to do household chores and be a team player, you're engaging them effectively in conversation and showing them that you respect their feedback. You can then teach them how to carry out their tasks so that you set them up for success instead of failure.

The age of the child doesn't matter. If this approach is carried out from toddlerhood to adulthood, not only will we harness or cultivate a great relationship with our children, we will teach them how to engage others effectively and how they should be engaged as they grow.

At the beginning of this transition from doing it all yourself to working as a team, consider creating a chore training manual. I know what you're thinking: you have no time as it is. But use the folks that have sacrificed their time before us and now share their findings on the Internet. Use Wikihow or mommy blogs, YouTube or other instructional platforms to begin assembling the best training manual for each task that you can find. If something is just close enough, modify it so that it fits your home perfectly. These manuals don't have to just be written – make a little video, take photos, be creative.

Next, schedule a training time with each child separately or, if you are planning on rotating chores, conduct a family group training. These exercises accomplish a couple of things if done right. For example, if you gamify it, you can have family time, training time, and chores happening all at once.

Gamify Chore Time

Here are a few ways to gamify your chore time:

1. Play Go Fish, trying to match socks coming out of the laundry;
2. Set a timer for a "10-minute tidy" and scramble as a family to tidy your assigned rooms;
3. Enjoy a family TV show and during commercial breaks race to get as much done as you can and try to finish your chores before the TV show comes to an end.
4. Battle of the Bedrooms! See Appendix B for rules.

The best part about gamifying chore time is that at the end, you have a clean house. And, if your children come back because "they don't remember" what to do or how to do it, guess what? They can refer back to the training documents and videos that you've stored in a very sacred and accessible place in your home.

The important thing to remember through all of this is that although about half of all businesses survive five years or longer, and about one-third survive ten years or longer, as mothers we don't have the luxury of failing. At the risk of sounding like your mother-in-law, your children are only little once. We only get eighteen trips around the sun with them in our homes if we are fortunate. I know that you know how important these years are, not just to them, but to you as well.

But let's talk about this just for a moment. We as mothers wait and wait and wait and dream of becoming mothers. Then, we're pregnant and we have all these grand plans on how we are going to be a certain kind of mother. Then the kid comes and all of a sudden it's not about us. Well, I am saying as loud as I can, *how you spend these years is absolutely about you too*! You are important and the type of mother you want to be is important and you should have that opportunity. There is no excuse! There is enough time. If you think you do not have enough time, I challenge you to have that talk with mothers who have angel babies. Now is the time to take control of yourself by relinquishing control over them. Which brings me to the partners.

There Are Many Ways to Load A Dishwasher

Is there really a right way to load a dishwasher? Yes. Oh yeah, for any partner that thinks they are off the hook in this book ... well ...not so fast... But I will challenge you, as spouses, to consider perspective. Working out of the home is hard. Working in the home is hard. One is not better or harder than the other. We all just have to accept that and respect the other's position.

That being said, you don't go to your partner's place of employment and try to do their job your own way. Why? Because processes for efficiency are already in place, tried and tested, and training has been done. A team of executives has already agreed this way is the absolute best way to do this job. They intentionally sought to create the most efficient system they could.

With that in mind, is your partner an executive decision-maker in the home as well? A marriage is a partnership and should be treated as such. The door swings both ways on this one. Husbands, if your wife has found an effective way to accomplish something within the home (or vice versa) that means that she's likely taken into consideration your hard-earned income and the most affordable and time-efficient way to complete that task for maximum results.

The two most sought-after commodities in this modern age are time and money. When you don't have enough time to accomplish something, you spend money to get it done. When you don't have enough money to accomplish something, you spend time on it instead. If one of you has a system that increases the efficiency of the workflows in your home, take that into consideration. The intention to do things efficiently and in a way that makes them fit with your work flow is what ultimately matters most. If your work flows are different, respect that. If something really does not fit the workflow of one partner, they need to be empowered to establish an efficient system given the same details and parameters.

Ultimately, as long as you are on the same page with the goal of intentionally working for maximum efficiency, you will reach the outcome you desire. As long as you desire the same outcome, is there a difference when it comes to how you achieve it? There are multiple ways to solve math equations, there are multiple ways to write a book. Why can't chores be done in multiple ways if the outcome is the same? This is not about controlling the process, but about bringing the vision to fruition in an efficient way. By relinquishing control over how things get done, you are actually taking back control of your time.

As funny as it is to say that your husband is your extra child, respect the fact that he's not. You two are a team and the tone of your household depends on the ability of upper management to get along, split the responsibilities, empower and embrace each other's thoughts so the house can be managed effectively.

The second is knowing that it's not mom and dad against the kids. Ultimately you are running one team. If there's something that isn't getting done continuously the problem has to be addressed at the root not with emotion but with logic and respect, and with an open mind seeking critical feedback from your other team members as well. After all, in any good company the best way to improve is for the CEO to continuously ask for feedback and make adjust accordingly.

If You Want Something Done Right ...

You can keep doing things yourself to get it done right, but where has it gotten you so far? If you're here, reading this book, it is likely that you are overwhelmed. If you are not overwhelmed by your current household status, put this book down right now, because I don't believe in wasting anyone's time. If you are overwhelmed and want to try something different, keep going.

After I found my purpose in life, I stopped focusing on micromanaging how other members of my household executed the tasks that were assigned to them. When I was living in my box full-time, I was so obsessed with the success inside my box that details like what side of the dishwasher the dishes were placed on ate away at me.

It was only when I finally realized what my mission was in life and I gave myself a greater purpose could I let my guard down and admit that the box was actually a hamster wheel.

I had been running in place and chasing the same cheese all this time because when I didn't catch it at the end of the day, (i.e. if I didn't have the perfect meal and a perfect house and all of the laundry folded and my home completely organized) then I felt as if I had failed for that day.

By seeing my husband as an equally respected director of the household and allowing my children the experience to learn what it takes to live in and care for a home, care for themselves, care for their family, and care for others I accomplished my real goal: raising a strong, happy and successful family.

⇆ Feedback From The Team

Here's what one of my kids had to say when I asked: What do we like about our household?

"I like that we get to help out around the house because you guys have a lot to do, carrying everything. You go to work during the day and Dad goes to work at night and you guys are just really busy. I guess I just like feeling helpful and useful. Not that I feel useless, but, like I said it makes me feel helpful and I like helping."

5:

Communications

*N*ow that you're starting to shift perspective and seeing your family as a team, it's important to look at how you communicate with one another.

It's not uncommon at all to have fights, arguments, or have to confront your husband or kids on an issue. No family is perfect. However, you don't have to be held hostage to an old communication paradigm, or a paradigm that holds a rigid "us versus them" or "I'm right / you're wrong" approach. With effective and skillful communication, you can turn even the nastiest arguments into teachable moments that end with both parties coming out smiling and hugging.

When it comes to having a positive confrontation with someone in the family, ask yourself first: what exactly is the issue? Let's look at an example: imagine that you would like your husband to communicate more. That's a challenge we all face at some point so let's pick this apart.

The communication style is bothering you because of a certain way that you are feeling. How are you feeling? Unloved, unappreciated, out of the loop? How do we confront this?

To start, does this really have anything to do with your husband? If we are only talking about how you feel it sounds like you have a standard for communication. The first step here is to manage your expectations and standards. In this case, you have an expectation when it comes to how you want your husband to talk with you, and he has a different expectation. When expectations are not in alignment, conflict is created.

Cheat Sheet

Positive Confrontation with someone in the family

1. Ask yourself first: what exactly is the issue?
2. How are you feeling?
3. How do we confront this?
4. As yourself, does this really have anything to do with the person in question?
5. Manage your expectations and standards.
6. Consider attaching a measurable unit to when and how you communicate with this family member.
   a. Are there a number of times you can check in with this person?
   b. What about a set length of time for these check-ins?
   c. Do you have practices to speak with each other in respectful and fair ways, even if in a heated argument?

d. If you have these in place, does the other person honor them?
e. Do you hold yourself to the same standard? Is it a reasonable expectation?
f. When the time comes to have this conversation, are you ready to effectively communicate your expectations and be willing to accept the other person's expectations?
g. What happens when they don't align?

In an example like this, where it's really more about how you feel about the communication than the issue itself, consider attaching a measurable unit to when and how you communicate with your partner. Are there a number of times you can check in with your partner? What about a set length of time for these check-ins? Do you have practices to speak with each other in respectful and fair ways, even if in a heated argument? If you have these in place, does your partner honor them? Do you hold yourself to the same standard? Is it a reasonable expectation? When the time comes to have this conversation, are you ready to effectively communicate your expectations and be willing to accept your spouse's expectations? What happens when they don't align?

For example, my husband and I have a weekly check-in which we refer to as a "week in review" where, over a cup of coffee, we discuss our successes, opportunities, finances, and future plans. If one of us doesn't think the other communicates frequently enough, we speak up about it.

I also have a rule before engaging in any confrontation: I determine what all of the possible worst-case scenario outcomes could be and consider how I might manage each of those situations so we can keep the interaction positive.

Having this rule in place keeps me, personally, from overreacting, especially if I have to address something that's driven with emotion. I say with confidence, emotional conversations had in the heat of the moment are never productive. Even if you walk away "winning" did you actually solve the problem? It's possible that the other person (even a small child) was just trying to manage your emotions by telling you what you want to hear.

Look Beyond The Emotion

There are ways to address a problem or thought process without being confrontational and yet still addressing it head-on. I encourage you to practice pausing when you are experiencing a reaction. By this I mean, rather than reacting to tone or body language, take a moment to try and see what's really at the root of the problem.

Often when our children (or spouses, or even ourselves) have a meltdown, the problem on the surface is not actually the problem, that's just the tipping point. Rather than reacting in a way that takes offense to tone or body language, really making a genuine effort to get to the root of the problem will actually help solve the problem. It will also avoid creating a snowball of emotions in which one party throws a fit and the other party takes defense.

As an example, recently I went on a field trip with my daughter, Lucy. The kids were in groups and Lucy was with a group of kids she had never met before. I noticed her body language change as early as two minutes into the trip. Her head was down, her feet were dragging. Worse, she was killing the vibe of the whole experience.

Rather than force or bribe her into being happier in that moment, I insisted we go back to the car. I explained to Lucy that we were there to have a good time and so were the other kids and one person bringing the vibe down wasn't fair to anybody. As I spoke, I could see Lucy growing increasingly frustrated.

When we got to the car, she exploded. She screamed, she cried, she spewed words that she didn't mean while I remained calm and waited for her emotions to play out. Once they had, I asked her what was really bothering her. When we started the day, she was in a great mood, excited to be on the field trip and obviously now that was not the case. Something had changed and we all saw it. She refused to answer, but not because she was being stubborn. It was because she didn't have the words to describe exactly what was wrong. She continued to be upset, so I asked her more detailed questions, ones that would allow me to deduce or at least get closer to the real answer. The more questions I asked, the closer I got to the truth. Lucy was upset that she wasn't in the same group as her friends. We talked about how it would be a great opportunity for her to meet new friends but she would have none of it, remaining upset.

Digging deeper in the conversation, I eventually discovered the real problem was that there was one friend in particular Lucy hadn't seen in a long time and she was looking forward to spending the day with her. Knowing this, I was then able to suggest we schedule a play-date privately.

More importantly than me understanding the root of her emotional frustration, Lucy got to understand what was driving her anger so that we could address it together. In addition, she could now identify it again if necessary, and communicate it effectively the next time without all that emotion.

Too often, when we're frustrated it's either because of a lack of communication or an unexplained expectation. In this case, Lucy's expectation was to hang out with her friend, and she didn't know how to communicate her strong feelings of disappointment when she couldn't. Rather than addressing her symptoms, her attitude, and her poor body language, we kept going until we hit the root of the problem.

When you are confronting the issue, look to heal the wound on the deeper level. Bringing awareness to this type of troubleshooting helps train your children to look beyond what's happening on the surface. When they have the ability and the maturity to do this, you'll find that there will be less hostility within the home because they're learning how to solve their problems in a more logical way rather than an emotional way.

Think back on all of those emotion-driven conversations. Did you have to address the issue again afterwards? If not, it's possible that you just struck fear into the heart of your opponent. That's no way to engage in any relationship: spouse, friend, child, co-worker, person on the street. The most fulfilling relationships are those that are equal in respect. Has anyone ever come at you with that much rage? How did you feel about them after? I don't think it was respect. It's more likely you had to be mindful of the way you engaged so you could keep them pacified. Did your parents ever yell at you for having an experience they didn't find suitable? What did you do? Did you have that experience again? If so, did you tell them about it? Chances are you didn't. And it was because you were taking their emotions into consideration and pacifying them.

There are ways to get past all of this, one of which is to pay close attention to your communication patterns and be keenly aware that this is an area in the home that needs to be tended to.

Communicate Effectively

Effective communication is really the key to a strong team. People thrive in their environment when they feel respected and important. There is a saying that we use in our home: speak to be heard, write to be understood, and listen to be a good communicator.

Tools to assist in communication:

1. Get it on the calendar.

   Schedule time to chat with *everyone* in your house. Forced communication may feel uncomfortable at first, but trust me it gets easier.

2. Have an agenda - and encourage the other person to have an agenda too!

   Having an agenda discourages any one person from hijacking the communication time. It is also a great habit for the kids to learn. No one likes a "dementor" (to use a Harry Potter term). You know, that person that sucks all of your emotional intelligence and doesn't think to ask how you've been. That is not a good habit to practice, and we want to practice positive habits as often as possible.

   Obviously, it's not a business meeting and shouldn't feel like one. Maybe your agenda is in a journal, maybe it's a scrapbook. Maybe you use pictures to guide the conversation. It could be a memories journal that you share. Bullet points or full sentences, both do just fine. The point is, cover all topics, especially the ones that you don't want to address or anything you need to confront. Address all of the "wins." We use headlines like, "Top Five Quotes of the Week" or a "Memory of the Week."

   Other ways to look at the wins include asking what each other's strengths were last week and what were some areas that we could have improved.

Often when things are going right, we just keep going. We only complain when something is wrong (another habit to avoid.)

3. Do personality assessments.

No, not the ones you see online in your social media news feed. There are real, proven tests that can help determine how someone else may want to be communicated with. For example, *The Five Love Languages* book will help you and your partner learn how you best express and receive love. The DiSC assessment is a tool for finding the top behavioral and personality traits of everyone in your household. You might even want to find a certified coach or study some of the dozens and dozens of personality profiling tests available.

Communication, after all, is not solely about talking, it's about listening and reciprocating. It's also about recognizing that each individual filters their information differently. By taking personality tests for the whole family, you'll come away with a stronger sense of how best to communicate to each individual within your family.

4. Set Personal Development Goals To Guide Your Responses.

Recall in chapter 3 I invited you to write down the meaning of life as a set of adjectives describing how you'd like to be. Well, in our household, this is a birthday tradition. Every birthday we pick who we'd like to be that year. You can keep the same adjectives or change them. But you have to commit to them for a year.

These words not only help you to stay on track with your vision and goals every day, but they affect your communication by giving you a guide for how to respond when faced with a choice or reaction. Every choice is an opportunity to be recognized as one of your adjectives. If after some practice you still aren't portraying a characteristic, study it. Go online, do some research. Get a book. Figure out ways to practice defining yourself.

Determining your adjectives is in itself a goal setting exercise as the words you choose are your goals. If you ask someone to describe you and they use those adjectives, congratulations! You've made your goal.

Consider common interactions as daily opportunities to make your goal. For example, if you use your manners frequently and consistently, you may be described as "polite." But if someone holds the door for you and you do not say thank you, you may lose that characteristic title. If you never used the term "I don't know" and instead used "I'll find out" you may then be considered intelligent or resourceful. And if either of those words are your chosen adjectives, then once again, congratulations! You made your goal.

Keep these goals in a place that can be easily viewed by the family. (They can be a fun art project too). Place them behind a pantry/closet door or similar common area. Instead of yelling or addressing behavioral issues, you can refer back to that guide to teach the difference between being happy and being moody, or being polite and being rude. I find there is a lot more buy-in from the kids especially because I am not telling them how to behave, rather I am reminding them how they would like to behave and their own personal goals.

5. Create a Coffee Chat Questionnaire.

Think of this as a "Your Opinion Matters" survey for the home. It could be a standard document that asks the same questions every time, like:

- Do you have any questions about your chores?

- How was dinner this week?

- Is there anything you would like to do this week together as a family or with your friends?

- If there was anything you could have changed last week what would it be?

These don't have to be conducted regularly, I mean it is a home for crying out loud. But if someone is really grumpy, moody or angry, these tend to help because they give family members a chance to be heard and reconnect to their feeling of belonging.

It's not really about the questions you ask. The idea is that it is opinion-based so your child knows that what they have to say matters. This is what will encourage them to open up to you about the things that really do matter.

By the way, this works well with your older kids, especially around the age that their friends may be the root of their stress, or you know, the feelings stuff: crushes, boyfriends, girlfriends, friends that hold hands. We were that age once too, I'm sure you remember what it was like.

6. Create a Schedule of Family Engagement Events.

Paper and digital calendars really are the best for the most efficient communication. Clear communication sets expectations, and clearly defined expectations make for more understood standards which means everyone knows their role and how to best fulfill it as a team member.

For families with more than one child I definitely recommend these types of tools because we've all heard those words, "They got more than me," or "That's so unfair." And even if they aren't saying it, they may be thinking it. Calendars will show you how much time is spent where, who picked the last movie, what the upcoming events are. They are a great way to analyze and justify guilt- free time for yourself too. I don't know about you, but if I go to the grocery store by myself, I feel guilty going to get a pedicure too. It feels like too much "me" time. With a visual on how much time gets delegated to your family, I guarantee your percentage of time for you is minuscule. Schedule your darn pedicure, put it on the calendar, and just do it!

7. Make A List of Fun Dinner Topics.

"How was your day?" gets old so fast. A great way to make dinner time fun and engaging is having some offbeat conversation starters. They can be anything from the basics to things like, "If you could meet anyone in the world, who would it be?" or, "If you were president what would you change?"

Here are a few more fun conversation- starting ideas:

1. If you had a spaceship what planet would you visit and what would you bring?
2. If you could invent anything what would it be and what would it do?
3. If you could meet a famous person who would it be and what would you talk about?
4. Where do you want to live when you grow up and why?
5. If you could drive right now where would you go and what would you drive?

Asking these types of fun questions at the dinner table creates a habit of being imaginative and interesting for the whole family while creating memories.

The Family That Communicates Together ...

If you haven't had the kind of life experience yet that perhaps offered you a glimpse of solid communication skills, it's well worth reading up on the topic. We communicate all the time, and we take it for granted that we are good communicators. All of the things I've addressed in this chapter, however, are things I've learned, through work and life. Taking the time to understand how everyone in your family uniquely communicates goes a long way to securing your foundation as a strong team. Practicing communicating in a non-reactive way and seeking to get to the heart of what's happening emotionally for yourself, your partner, and your kids, will yield profound outcomes. When we are not communicating consciously and with intention we are just perpetuating dynamics and reinforcing poor communication habits. Take the time, read a few books if you need to, try new things, and include the whole family as you develop the communication skills required of a seriously bad-ass Chief Executive Mom.

⇆ Feedback From The Team

Here's what one of my children had to say when I asked:

Do you feel like your opinion matters?

"Yes, I know it does. And I like that you force me to talk about things because it makes me feel better afterwards."

6:

The Accounting Department

Your internal Accounting Department, of which you are the Department Manager, is a fundamentally crucial department in Your Household, Inc. Financial wellness is the root of how we operate.

Let's face it, we live in a time where we need money to secure our basic needs and we want money to indulge in luxuries. How we manage our finances determines how quickly we are able to react to wants, needs and circumstances.

One thing I've learned about money is that it's never an issue when you have enough of it, and a large or small salary is not necessarily the deciding factor in how much money you keep. It's actually a balance of earnings and expenditures. Continuously having the money talk or feeling chronically stressed about your financial situation are really signs of poor money management, which can be a hard truth to swallow. Please know this: if this is you, don't feel bad! You can learn and it's never too late. I don't know about you but unless you took in-depth accounting classes, it's entirely likely you were taught zero money management skills in school. Traditionally, at least since the turn of the 20th century, money management has been left to parents to pass onto their kids.

When it comes down to it, what we really need to survive is food, water, and a roof over our heads. Everything else we have to accept as a want. Do we need 500 thread count sheets? No. Do we want them? Yes. Do we need a big screen TV on the wall (or a TV at all)? No. Do we want it? Yes.

The task at hand is really one of evaluating what our wants and needs are, and how we are spending. Partners should want the same things. If they're not on the same page generally, life and finances will be more difficult. Period.

Yet it's not compromise that most couples need, it's committing to a greater goal.

It is this commitment to a shared vision that makes for a strong relationship. Compromise implies that someone is sacrificing what they want to make somebody else happy; what I really want is to have a good marriage and a household that is functioning and happy as a result. By not compromising with our spending and being on the same page, we create great habits with money that eventually translate into great habits in our relationship.

We develop habits more quickly with money because we work with it more frequently than with anything else. Developing good money habits by being con-scious about every expenditure will lead to good decision-making and habits becoming second nature, which is useful when it comes time to make big spend-ing decisions.

Keep in mind, the financial person in the household is not necessarily the person who brings in the most income. Instead, it is the person with the patience to check into the bank accounts and all of the accounts payable and the organizational skills and discipline to make sure that everything is paid on time along with the ability to ensure money is left over for savings.

When I stayed home full-time my husband worked and I paid all of the bills. Although I work now, I still over-see all the bills. Just because we are both working does not mean that we split every department equally in half. Instead we play to each other's strengths and take over respective departments to be sure they are managed appropriately, much like how the head chef of a restau-rant does the cooking, and not the accounting.

The important point is that each of these areas should be recognized as its own job. Just because you are the homemaker doesn't mean that you should be doing all of the jobs and just because one person may be the breadwinner doesn't mean that they should be doing all of the finances. Communicate and be aware of each other's strengths and how each weakness can either be outsourced or delegated to a different family member. When our son's chore was to wash the dishes, the dishes were always dirty. When we switched it up and trusted him with managing trash and recycle, wastebaskets were always empty. It's vital to assign, observe, evaluate, and reassign when appropriate.

Managing Your Accounts

I don't necessarily encourage separate personal accounts for one person or another. My advice for you if you wish to have multiple accounts is to set up a savings account in a different bank with no debit card and no checks for accessibility, and one account out of which you pay all the bills. Other than that, with whatever leftover money you have, you can either choose to open separate accounts or maintain one joint account; the choice is yours.

I do, however, recommend for children to open their own personal accounts so they can start practicing good financial decisions at a young age. Lots of banks have kids savings accounts that can be opened as young as age eight, and by the time your child is fourteen they can have a bank account with more services. As much as Mark and I tried to teach our children about good spending habits we found that they learned best by experience. If they can learn with smaller monetary amounts now, they will have already made many of the silly mistakes that most of us make when we are young adults and when the consequences are more severe.

Again, it's important for mom and dad to be on the same team financially because this practice emphasizes strong communication and an awareness of each other's needs. This, in turn, will trickle down into every other facet of the relationship resulting in a stronger team.

Something else you'll want to do is sit with your significant other once per month to offer a breakdown of where you are financially. Sharing financial information is important in a relationship. Why? Because no one person should be controlling another, and money is a key factor in how you conduct your day-to-day life. Should you share your money? That's up to you. But at the very least, share the information.

No matter who is in charge of the finances, it's up to that person to create and manage the budget. In my experience, budgets work and are extremely useful when it comes to helping you stretch your dollar in the most effective way. So, let's take a look at setting up your budget.

Your Home Budget

If you have not done so already, go to the back of the book to take a look at some examples of a home budget binder in the Appendices. This tool or one similar will be crucial to your success in managing your finances.

You don't need a special home office for your Accounting Department, and if you already have a file cabinet, throw it out. Unless you own a home-based business, there is no need for a large file cabinet. All that you require is a fireproof locked box, a small one, and a binder.

You may be thinking, "Well, I have really important things filed—that's why they're filed." Yes, if you didn't think they were important, you wouldn't have filed them. I can assure you however, that no less than eighty percent of what's in your file cabinet can be donated to the trash at this very moment. If you are freaking out a little over even the thought of purging those papers, that's okay. We'll get there in my later chapter on decluttering.

Inside your budget binder the first sheet should be the "Profit & Loss Statement." This document will have all of your household expenses itemized, as well as asset forms, like all of your utilities, medical bills, mortgage documents, bank statements, and pay stubs (if applicable) I have included a sample Profit and Loss statement you can see or copy for your own use in Appendix C.

Behind that form you can then put all those bills and statements for the most current month. If you do not have a three-ring hole punch, use an insert with a pocket or a sheet protector to store. On an ongoing basis, whenever those documents come in through the mail, place them behind the budget form.

Schedule yourself 10 minutes per week to maintain your binder and three hours per month to pay all your bills and fully analyze your finances.

After you've written everything into your budget sheet, add it up to see what your monthly expenses are. Take into consideration recurring expenses and one-time expenses. Is that number what you thought it would be? Do this for three months to determine your cash flow, basically the difference between how much you spent and how much you earned for that month.

Why is this important first? Because determining your cash flow will help you identify whether or not you should outsource. Again, this budget sheet is a profit and loss statement. Simply identify every dollar spent: every recurring expense, every one-time expense, utilities, etc. and subtract that from your top line revenue (your income). Your bottom line (the difference) will help you determine if you are operating your house in the positive or negative.

Once you know if your cash flow is positive or negative, you can look at where you want to spend more time or more money. If you would like a more positive cash flow, for example, you might cut expenses for things you can do yourself; i.e. if you hire a landscaper, consider doing your own gardening and mowing instead. Or, if you eat out a lot, take more time to cook. On the contrary, if you have positive cash flow but would like more time, you can now look at outsourcing everyday tasks by hiring an affordable helper.

Next, write down both long-term and short- term financial goals for the family. Keep this information in the binder or in a visible place for daily viewing. Keeping your financial vision accessible like this helps you stay focused on your financial goals. I wrote earlier about the daily to-do and putting items on the to-do list to get you closer to your goals. Well, if your long-term goal is to save $10,000 in a year, then "save $27.40" (or $10,000 divided by 365 days) should be on your daily to do-list as a short-term goal.

After you have done this process you may still want to know where your money is going. If you are Excel-savvy, you will enjoy sorting your spreadsheet to show you what you've spent each month (and see Appendix C for an example spreadsheet you can copy and use for your monthly expense tracking). An easier route, if you use credit for most purchases, is to review your credit card statements, where they will have divided your spending by category.

As a side note, get into the habit of checking all of your statements, regardless of whether you're looking to see what categories you spend most in. I can't emphasize this enough—and don't be afraid to check, either! Knowing your numbers is the direct path to money management smarts. Don't keep your head in the sand.

List your expenses, track your expenses, categorize your expenses, and get the snapshot of how your money is being spent. This is the single best way to make better choices going forward.

From here, you can create your budget in a realistic way, making it a budget that allows you to meet the needs of your family while also contributing towards your financial goals.

Once you've created your family budget, you can share it with your kids and let them have a hand in planning. In our family, our older three participate with our planning. We take them to the store together and make a game out of who could find the item at the best price. We have taught them to consider the quantity of what they are purchasing compared to the price of the item to determine the unit value. It's amazing how much they will learn and retain when they are able to put their winning item in the basket for check out. This type of hands-on shopping with the kids teaches them to look past branding and conveniences and to look deeper for quality and sensible budget. As I mentioned earlier, it's really up to parents to educate their kids when it comes to money management, at least until schools change their curriculum (some of which are starting to). Even if your kids are learning money management in school, it's important to give them the opportunity to practice and experience successful spending habits and the consequences of hasty spending. The better you become at setting and adhering to budgets, the better a role model you are for your kids.

It's 9 p.m., Do You Know Where Your Money Is?

I'm going to take you on a brief diversion here, but this is a topic worthy of attention. Just now, we were talking about categorizing your expenses so you can get a handle on where your money is going. I cannot tell you how many families I know that burn money by eating out. In fact, food is among the biggest expense people have, and I bet you still don't even think that food expenses can make such an impact. Believe me—they do, especially if you're not paying attention.

I have a couple of hard and fast financial rules that I follow and feel would be beneficial to share with you.

1. Do not go out to eat, unless you've been planning it for a week.
2. If it's over $20 and wasn't researched, drop it and run out of the store.
3. Save $10,000 first, then save for your vacation (and do so every time).

Rule #1: Eating Out Eats Your Budget

One of the biggest mistakes we make in our fast-paced culture is letting our emotions and appetites control us. Rather than allowing this to happen, try to make going out to eat (even if it's a fast food stop) a goal instead of an act of desperation. If you truly want to be in control of your finances, you need to be in control of your appetite. I dare you to go back and see what your most consistent, largest, unknown expense is. I can probably tell you without looking—it's food.

When we're too busy, we go out to eat. When we're bored, we go out to eat. When we want to connect with someone, we go out to eat. Why can't we just make a good home-cooked meal? Is it that there isn't enough time? Or is it really that we are overlooking it as a priority?

Tips for eating out in a financially sound way:

- Plan it ahead of time. This gives you a finish line.
- Be strategic in your timing. What is the maximum time you've gone without eating out? Can you hit

that time frame plus one day (yes, Starbucks counts too)? If you can't, rework your strategy until you are down to once every other week. And consider this: if you swing by a coffee shop every weekday for a year and buy the cheapest black coffee, no frills, that's $517.40. If you buy that same bag, served the same way and make it from home, it's about $40—for the *year*. That's for the $1.99 coffee, chances are you're spending much more every time. And if you do like the fancy coffee, there is no reason that you can't make it at home (there are cheap stovetop espresso makers that the Italians have been using for centuries that produce quality espresso). That extra $480 or so could have bought you a weekend getaway where they serve fabulous coffee. And this is just applying the least expensive eating out expense that you'll have!

Really, I challenge you to do the math or call me and I'll do the math with you. Not eating out saves the most money, period. And when you do have the opportunity to do it, you can go as big or as fancy as you'd like because you've earned that experience.

Rule #2: If it's over $20 and wasn't researched, drop it and run out of the store.

This is a tough one. I was once struck by these wise words from a college professor I had: "A want only becomes a need when the consumer has the buying power." In other words, you only turn your wants into needs when you have the money to buy them. Such a profound statement—and another invitation to take a closer look at what you perceive your wants and needs really are.

Being clear on your wants and your needs really requires ignoring mass marketing and using a little superpower I refer to as "common sense." As an example, I had a friend that was having her third baby. She had an SUV with no payment, and that suited her family perfectly. As soon as she found out she was pregnant with the third, she rushed out and bought a minivan, because in her mind they *need*ed it. Hearing her constantly complain about money, I asked her if they could sit tight a little longer before committing to a payment like that. She replied, "No, we definitely *need* the minivan. If we don't buy one, I'll have to go out and buy new car seats so they all fit, and car seats are so expensive now."

I found this astonishing. The most expensive car seat I could find online was $569. Multiply that times three, it brings you $1707. While that is pricey, it's nothing compared to the $25,000 price tag of a minivan!

The reality is that our needs really boil down to a roof over our heads with functioning utilities, basic hygiene products, enough food to remain healthy, water, and minimal appropriate clothing. Everything else can be considered a want and we must recognize them as such.

My husband and I keep this rule to help us keep from making emotionally-driven or unnecessary expenditures: If it costs more than $20 and you didn't go to the store with the intention to buy it, leave it. Go home and research it online. Read the reviews, check prices, put it on your calendar to go back in a week to purchase it. If you make it back to the store and are an educated consumer, you have earned your purchase. If not, put the money you would have spent on it into your savings account. Or, if you are already a good saver, put it into your "fun money" envelope. Either way, you've used sense with your finances.

Rule #3: Save $10,000 first, then save for your vacation.

I know, you think this is impossible. I suggest $10,000 as the magic number here because it is realistic to save when it's broken down daily. When you break it down by the day it's only $27.40/ day for one year. Still feel high to you? Well, if you are a family of four and you're about to eat out at a restaurant, chances are you're spending at least double that amount. If you get a coffee from a coffee shop five days a week it will also equal that amount. If you go to Target and leave with more than you planned it is likely that you could have shaved $27 off of that trip as well.

I like the number 10,000 because it will likely be a great emergency fund, and it will get you past the intimidation of saving five figures. Most of us like to think we are living inside of our means, but the reality is the majority of middle-class American families are living well outside of their means and classifying additional purchases as needs. The only thing you *need* is confidence in your long-term vision, success, security, a solid foundation, and a large enough number to give you the confidence to realize that you can not only save that amount of money, you can save it without feeling too much of the pinch.

I'll share with you how I did it. When my older three kids where six, four, and two-years-old, I wanted desperately to take them to Disney World. I remember the conversation as we were driving away from a fast food drive-thru, I asked my husband when he thought would be a good time of the year to take them; when did he think he could get off work and where should we stay. I could see him getting frustrated as I pressed him on the topic. Finally, he said, visibly stressed, "I don't think it's the right time to go on vacation!"

I explained that the kids were at the perfect ages for their first trip to Disney. We went back and forth for about ten minutes before I finally asked how much he wanted to have saved before we could talk about it again. He blurted out $10,000, thinking that might scare me out of having the conversation ever again. Instead, I saw it as a challenge.

I went home and cut costs everywhere I could. That was the last unplanned fast food drive-thru we ever went through. I figured out how much I needed to save weekly and set up an automatic transfer on every payday to transfer that amount to a bank account that we had no online access to. Every two months I found myself visiting that bank to check in on how we were doing.

Here are some of the areas where I cut costs:

- We stopped buying ready-made snacks and pre-pared foods at the grocery store;
- Instead of each person getting their own favorite ice cream, we got the five-gallon tub of Neapolitan;
- I bought meat in bulk and made multiple meals out of it by portioning it into freezer safe bags.
- I shopped at consignment stores when necessary.
- I also found that by shopping online I not only saved on generally cheaper items, I also saved extra money I would have otherwise spent just by hanging out at my favorite superstores. (How many times have I gone shopping for toilet paper only to leave with a cartful of things I thought we might need but could have lived without?)

By the end of the year the amount of money I saved, plus our tax return, matched the five-figure challenge. Sure enough, on February 21st of that year, we drove down to Disney.

To Allowance Or Not To Allowance

A lot of parents question whether or not to give allow-ances to their kids, and this is another area that is really personal to you and your family. In our house-hold, allowance is not given out of entitlement, instead, allowances are awarded after the work has been com-pleted and invoices have been issued just like in real life (we taught our kids how to write invoices to keep tabs on what's owed to them). We have a checklist for each of the kids that is maturity and strengths appropriate. After they have completed five of those checklists at one hundred percent, one for each work day, they earn fifty percent of their age in allowance.

We believe that allowance should be given based on duties and work ethic, just like in real life. Therefore, if our kids go above and beyond with their checklists and take on extra tasks or pay special attention to detail they then receive seventy-five percent of their age as an incentive. It doesn't break the bank and it keeps them motivated to be a productive member of the household while learning both the freedom and the burden of collecting a paycheck.

While we also teach the kids good practices on how they could save their money, spend their money, and donate to their favorite charities, the final outcome is solely determined by them. It has been interesting to watch how each child is so unique in their money management: we have one child that's a terrific saver, one that's a moderate spender and one that is always broke (but she is learning!) Our littlest one is now four years old and has just begun earning. She enjoys very much going to the dollar store to pick out a new box of crayons, and already doesn't like when she doesn't have any money left.

It is helpful to give kids this freedom to explore money and there's really no reason not to let kids get learning about money from an early age. As long as we are existing in this economic paradigm, giving your kids money tools as soon as you can will only set them up for success down the road.

Holidays

Another potential money sinkhole in our lives are holidays, especially Christmas. During the most expensive times of the year, (which pretty much runs from November 1 all the way to January 1 nowadays) it's really easy to get caught up in the retail hype. From decorations to gifts, the pressure to show someone how you feel through a wrapped box or bag can drain your bank account very quickly.

How to stay sane and keep your money close throughout all of this? Remember, it is the thought that counts. Every time you try to match or top a gift, you are just upping the ante for next season. It's not just hurting you, it's hurting the other person as well. Instead, take the guesswork out and try to start a new tradition. For instance, my sister gives me toe socks for Christmas every single year since year, and has since I was ten years old. Do I need toe socks at thirty-five? No, But I look forward to keeping our tradition alive every year and it costs her less than ten dollars. Your traditions don't have to be specific per person either. My stepmother bakes assorted cookies and sweets and writes everyone's name on their gingerbread man in icing. We cherish her thoughtfulness and it's a tradition we all look forward to each year.

> *Evaluate your finances, spend with intention, and save the rest.*

It really is that simple. If you don't go on vacation for a year or two, that's okay. When you need to relax and take your deserved time off from work, you can have a stay-cation, or source local activities to give your family the feel of a get-away without necessarily dropping the amount of money most vacations require. When you finally do take that vacation, you'll feel that much more accomplished that you saved your way to it and still have savings left over for that rainy day.

The older I get, the sillier it sounds when I hear a twenty-one year-old say, "I'm so old." The same holds true for the person that spends like crazy and has the nerve to say, "I'm so broke," or even for that person to think that way. If you are not homeless and have the ability to work (either inside the home our outside), then there is absolutely no reason for you to barely make ends meet. Now is the time to get your financial shit together. No excuses.

⤷ Feedback From The Team

Here's what one of my kids had to say when I asked:
Are you okay with you buying your own things and budgeting when we go to the store?
"I think it's good for us because if we spend something and find something else and you have no money, it

doesn't feel good. If you find something and you think you might want it you should think about it before you get it. You don't want to do it right away because if you find something else that you want after you pay for it then you won't have enough money to get it. Like try and see which toy you're going to play with more and not leave behind after five minutes."

7:
Department of Food & Beverage

After you have a handle on your financial health, your eating habits are next on the list. As I mentioned, food is likely the biggest expense that you are unaware of.

Along with being Chief Executive Mom, chances are you are also the Director of Food & Beverage at Your Household, Inc. You are running a kitchen! Even if you aren't the only one cooking, you are still the person who:

- Plans the menu
- Shops for the inventory
- Is responsible for the execution of meals
- Is likely in charge of the condition of the kitchen and all its components

The emphasis in this chapter will be on meal planning, and you'll need a couple of things to get started: a calendar, a shopping list (I like Wunderlist), the budget, and any requests from the family. Oh, and Pinterest, just in case.

For years, I used a large desktop calendar because it had enough lines for me to squeeze in breakfast, lunch, and dinner. I would put the current month right onto the refrigerator with some magnets. The kids were just old enough to read and they loved it. I would include them in the process for a few minutes each so they were able to identify and look forward to the days that we were having "their" favorite meal. I would, of course, give them options to choose from so they would stay close to our pantry ingredients.

Here is an example of their basic breakfast menu options:

1. Eggs
2. Yogurt
3. Oatmeal
4. Fruit & Toast
5. Cereal

All these categories were placed weekly on the calendar in kid-chosen order (with no duplicates). Saturdays were reserved for Mom-Made Special Breakfast while Sundays were reserved for Dad to do the same. Now that my kids are older, one weekend day is their turn to cook.

You may be thinking, my kid(s) doesn't like some of those things. Or, maybe you aren't crazy about some of those things. Like everything else in this book, the above-mentioned categories are just suggestions, feel free to modify them to fit your household. But hear this: when you continuously repeat meals—or anything for that matter—the fun gets sucked right out of it. It's important to change it up a bit. Even though that list is basic, there are many different ways to put a spin on the ingredients. There are at least twelve ways to cook an egg all on its own, and that's not including the sides you can put with it. So, be sure to change it up as often as possible.

By having a calendar visually accessible to all, rather than your kids dreading their meal for the day, they can look forward to "their day" and trust me, using this angle will make them complain much less! This goes for all meals. Spread them out, mix them up, use favorites and remix the favorites.

Next, I plan "dinner." I use quotation marks because we don't really do "dinner" as our main meal in the evening. Our heavier, or main, meal is closer to the middle of the day, and our evening meal is lighter (we like to take it easy on our digestive systems late in the day). If you don't homeschool your kids or you live too far from the school for your kids to be able to come home for lunch you can still send them to school with a hearty lunch by using thermoses and Tupperware. You can also consider having a portioned plate ready for your kids to eat immediately after school. This approach is about ensuring there is adequate time for digestion before sleep. And if it feels like you risk losing "family time" which traditionally is found at dinner, you can always have a light snack in the evening which can be the "family meal" experience. Remember, every family is unique and this is one area in which you can really be creative.

Personally, I also like to plan my calendar by mixing up ways to cook and themed days. For example:

Sundays - Cook on the BBQ;
Mondays - Slow Cooker/QuickPot Day
Tuesdays - Soup, sandwich, and/or salad
Wednesdays - Remix day;
Thursdays - Cultural dishes;
Fridays - In-home "take-out"
    (i.e instead of ordering pizza, make it yourself!)
Saturdays - Casseroles.

Now, saying our weeks are themed sounds cool, like you're really creative. But the real reason we theme our week around a cultural dish is so that we can easily recycle the ingredients.

For Italian week, for instance, I'll do breaded chicken parmesan with angel hair pasta and red sauce. The secret is to bulk cook the ingredients, so I'll make the whole meal on a Sunday afternoon. Then, I'll use that breaded chicken sliced thin for salads on Tuesday. I'll use the angel hair pasta for Pasta Alfredo on Wednesday for Remix Day. On Friday, maybe we make mini pizzas since we already have red sauce and cheese. I might do meatballs on Monday for the slow cooker and use them with the pasta or make meatball subs.

By the end of the week, you'll have burned through all your ingredients without burning a hole in your pocket. It's a resourceful way of using food (and Remix day is a clever way to use up leftovers.)

After big meals like the ones I mentioned, I plan for something light in the evening, like veggies and hummus, fruit salad, or a light sandwich.

Planning the whole food calendar for the month all at once also helps to balance the weight of your meals. On a soup and salad day, I'll plan a heavier sandwich for the evening; on days I know everyone will be sustained from lunch, I will put out a fruit, veggie, or cheese tray for us to eat in the evening.

Another quick trick for days when your schedule is overwhelming is smoothies. Smoothies can be very easily prepped, they store nicely in the freezer, and can be consumed guilt-free because you are using fresh fruits and veggies. They are wonderful on the go and kids usually love them!

Meal Planning Is Cost-Effective

Ask anyone working in the nutrition space and they will tell you: meal planning is incredibly cost effective and efficient.

If you practice meal planning based on one core dish per week and expanding on those ingredients throughout the rest of the week you will essentially starve your pantry. When our family of six starves our pantry our trip to the grocery store is around $175. That amount of fresh, non-processed foods will make a week's worth of breakfast, lunch, dinner and a snack just before bedtime. That equals about $25 per day divided by our family of 6 which is about $1.04 per person per meal.

For our same family of six, eating out at a moderately priced quality fast food establishment is at least $5 per person. If we continue that trend and eat out for every meal, spending $5 per person each time, our weekly bill would be $840.

Essentially, we are either trading time for money or money for time. A meal that will cost us a little more time to prepare will cost less money to assemble, and a meal that will cost us virtually no time to prepare will likely cost five times as much in ingredients.

Make Meal Planning Work For You

When do you do all of this? And how do you do all of this? The answer: with discipline and recruits. Pick one day and make your planning session as non- negotiable as your sleep. Schedule it in your calendar, put your phone on Do Not Disturb, put headphones in, and get it done. As long as meal prep is for seven days, you can do it any day of the week. There is no rule that says it has to be Sundays.

Also, be sure to work your food shopping time into your plan. I personally do not do the grocery shopping on the same day I prepare the meal because it's just too draining. We don't want exhaustion, we want balance. Also, it's okay to outsource. Remember, you are the Director of Food. If you happen to do the shopping, prep, and cooking, that's fine. But respect that each of those jobs are different and can be outsourced to your spouse or kids (depending on their age), food shopping services or personal home assistants.

Cut yourself some slack if you can't get it done in a day—you are doing the work of at least four people. Space it out and pace yourself accordingly. If you overdo it, you're going to get overwhelmed and hate it, and never want to do it again. Breaking down the tasks— planning, shopping, preparing—and spacing them out will put you on track for balance.

Kids In The Kitchen

I can't say this enough: recruit your children! They will find it fun for a minute, and then they might hate it, and then they'll love it, and then not so much. They're kids for crying out loud.

Still, there are multiple life lessons here when you give your kids the opportunity to join you in the kitchen:

1. They get to learn how to cook and navigate a kitchen, both skills they will greatly appreciate as adults.
2. They get to own their role as a key member of the household.
3. They continue learning financial responsibility. If you take them to the store and show them the difference between low unit prices and how to shop

for a good price and not just the sale price, they will learn very quickly about budget.

4. They get to make memories with you and build your bond. Consider twenty years from now: will they say, "My mom cooked for us," or will they say, "My mom taught us how to cook"?

Isn't that the appreciation piece we're working towards? Aren't we the ones that set them up for success? It doesn't just apply to college or scholastics. That's life. Your kids could grow up to be super successful with an above-average salary but if they don't have basic life skills to help them manage their money, they will be unhappy and broke.

These are the skills that we forget to ingrain in our kids: basic survival. Just because we have the convenience of ready-made food around us, doesn't mean we shouldn't at least know how to cook, or exercise our ability to live within a budget. Especially when this process will allows more time for lasting memories and instill life lessons. It's not going to be easy at first, but neither is working out, or algebra, or anything worth achieving. As they say: "Today's work out is tomorrow's warm-up"

The process of preparing a meal; the cleaning, chopping, seasoning, and cooking; these are processes that bring the family together. They are, in a sense, constant opportunities for team-building, morale boosting, and hands-on training.

The moment a child expresses interest in participating is the moment we give the responsibility. Our youngest, Nora, four years old, has plastic knives she uses to cut tomatoes. Meanwhile our oldest, Vanessa, twelve years old, is often in charge of cooking the proteins. All kids are different and mature differently. What matters is that the kitchen gives us an amazing venue to teach, bond, and socialize in ways that are completely lost when we start introducing unhealthy, processed foods into our diet.

Build Your Kitchen Team

Here are some things you can invite your kids to do in the kitchen to help them feel a part of your team while allowing them to build their kitchen skills.

Age 2
- Wash their own fruit
- Get their own water from a pitcher with a spout.
- Help themselves to pre-made and pre-measured snacks (i.e. Ziploc™ bags of grapes and cheese, baby carrots, etc.)
- Make simple sandwiches, i.e. toast and jam

Ages 3-4
- Use a plastic knife to cut fruit and vegetables
- Crack and scramble eggs
- Make sandwiches with two or more ingredients (i.e. deli sandwiches, peanut butter and jam)

Ages 5-7

- Use the microwave
- Make popcorn
- Their first knife license (a paring knife)
- At this age, training with knives can begin, as can making more complete meals, i.e. not just eggs, but eggs, toast, and coffee

Ages 8-11

- Prepare and cook carbs such as rice, mashed potatoes and pasta
- Prepare and cook vegetables and other side dishes on the stove top
- Add bacon, pancakes, and oatmeal or grits to breakfast
- Start learning to bake. (Note: using measuring cups to cook will also help them understand fractions)

Ages 12 and up

- Understand at what temperature proteins should be cooked;
- Effectively cook a full meal, start to finish.

The way I see it, the Department of Food & Beverage should always be recruiting. The kitchen is full of amazing life lessons for your children to learn. You don't have to be the chief cook and bottlewasher. Let your team in on the action. Delegate according to strengths and maturity and be willing to train them for success.

⇆ Feedback From The Team

Here is what one of my kids had to say when I asked them: What is your favorite grown-up thing to do?

"Cooking. I cook eggs: fried, scrambled, eggs in a basket, never sunny side up, I've cooked soft boiled eggs. I also know how to make fresh broth with noodles in it. I make pancakes with special ingredients. I cannot tell the world my special ingredients."

Organization within the Organization

Prior to team training on keeping an organized, clean home, it's time to train the trainer on the three-step method I use to optimize systems for chore execution. In the next three chapters, we will take the 3-step methodology and apply it directly to our work organizing, sorting, purging, and establishing a healthy chore routine.

The 3-step methodology (see Appendix A) is made up of these three core skills:

- decisiveness
- insightfulness
- consistency

In this chapter, we'll really get clear on the importance of decisiveness. And nowhere else is there a better invitation to be decisive than in decluttering. Let's get started!

There are a few questions to consider before we get into optimal systems for chore execution.

First, is your house cluttered?
Second, is it organized?
Third, is your work flow effective in your home?

Whether or not we realize it, there is something calming about order. It's part of the reason we like music; it's repetitive and predictable. Our brains tend to like things that are predictable because we know what's coming next. When you have something that's unpredictable or something rocks your world a little bit it creates a sort of chaos which sparks low to high levels of anxiety. Consider when you are driving and the driver in the next lane moves in front of you with no blinker to warn you. Can you feel the road rage?

In the case of a cluttered or messy home, there is a feeling of unpredictability which contributing with contributes to a latent sense of anxiety in you and your family members. When you are chronically unable to find things because they did not get put back into the right place, you start wasting time looking and looking, and soon enough that means someone is late for work because they couldn't find their keys. This kind of chaotic atmosphere is avoidable when you create a space that has order—and order that addresses your unique family's needs and workflow.

A house that is lacking in order is usually one filled with clutter, so let's start there.

There are plenty of resources, books, blogs, articles that teach a variety of methods to de-clutter. One of my favorites is the Marie Kondo method from her book, *The*

Life-Changing Magic of Tidying Up. In the book, the author does a fabulous job bringing awareness to our emotional attachment with our things. The long and the short of her approach is that if something brings you joy when you hold it, keep it. If it doesn't "spark joy" you toss it.

At my company, Assistant Pro, we've built our methods for purging around a similar theory.

For example, both Marie Kondo and I advocate for decluttering before organizing, and we both agree that the person should hold the item and attune to the feeling it brings. We also both do memorabilia last. Where I differ in my approach is that I invite each individual in a household to tackle their own items.

If you are living in a cluttered home, like to have a lot of stuff, and already feel the anxiety bubbling up even reading this far, just take a breath. I'm with you, and you can do this. Let's dive in.

Sort And Purge

Sorting and purging are the best first steps to take when it comes to decluttering and organizing. This is because when you organize, you're categorizing and setting the standard for where things will live going forward. If you do that first, you're actually organizing things you might not want or need. Thus, before you get to see your closet organized, clean, pretty and color-coordinated from left to right top to bottom you must do the sorting and purging first.

Sorting and purging are not necessarily about throwing things away as much as they are about making a decision. Think about it this way: it might be easier to look at a pile of papers and just organize them by putting them into a neat pile on the side of the desk, but taking the time to make decisions around what to keep and what to toss is actually the more effective first step. If you throw away the entire pile you risk throwing out something important, whether it's a social security card or an unpaid bill. Rather than confronting the clutter, you just want to organize it but this is a premature approach.

We're going to address sorting and purging the same way we are learning to address all other areas of our processes: Systematically.

If you are going to work through your whole house, this is the order I recommend: clothes first, then paperwork, then additional problem areas (kitchen/bathrooms), then memorabilia last.

I always start with the bedroom because it should be your sanctuary, your peaceful place. When you fall asleep each night it should be with a calm mind in a clear, organized space. When you wake up, your room should be at peace. If you can't find your clothes, shoes, belt, or mascara at the beginning of your day, you're setting yourself up for a chaotic day. Keep in mind, chaos is the natural order of the world. Anything that can go wrong will. Whether we realize it or not, we are constantly fighting against small bits of chaos that may ensue around us. Our way of fighting that chaos is its direct nemesis: organization. To be organized means to plan and live purposefully with intent. Starting your morning poorly sets a negative tone for the day.

Try to make sure the laundry is done beforehand and pull out any stored clothing that is only worn season- ally. When I say everything, I mean every tank top. It doesn't matter if it's worn all the time. Even if you think you aren't going to throw them away or you wear that top often, bring it out anyway. Take those shirts off the hangers, get them out of the laundry, even get the ones from storage.

Once you've pulled everything out, place all the clothes on the center of your bed. Dig through and pick out one of *those* shirts. The one that makes you feel the best when you wear it. The one that makes you feel warm and fuzzy on the inside and makes you exude confidence on the outside—you know the shirt I'm talking about.

It's really important that you pick that particular shirt up and hold it. Now, you might chuckle a little because this is the part where I tend sound a little bit crazy, but this is totally true and it works. Give it a try!

Everything evokes a feeling, even your clothing. When you pick out that one thing you love so much, you are attaching a feeling to it and setting the tone for your purge session by already connecting with what makes you happy.

Hold that "happy" shirt and connect with the feeling that it brings up. Now put it down and pick up another. Within three seconds you will know if that shirt brings you the same exact feeling.

I use a rule of three during this process. If you have three shirts in a row that go into the "happy" pile, put all three back into the original pile, hold your "happy" shirt again for three full seconds, and then re-evaluate those tops again. By doing this, you are reminding your brain and your body what the objective is: find only the happiest shirts you own.

Now you have one—and only one—item and you can leave it front and center. This is one item that you know for sure creates happiness and gives you that special, empowered, confident feeling.

Now that you have your *thing*, you're going to divide the pile into two categories: clothes that give you this good feeling, and clothes that don't. Don't panic! We're not throwing that other pile away, we're just using process of elimination as we make decisions on what stays and what goes.

Again, this is not a garbage pile. This is just a pile that doesn't give you the feeling. If you feel like it's a staple item (something practical, though, not emotional) and you must have it because it's a white top and you need it for work, it's okay to put it in this pile. We're going to go through it again, but first we want to get out all the important stuff, all the things that leave you feeling cheerful.

Deciding between pile one and pile two should be a split-second decision. Maybe you'll go through the first set of things a little bit reluctantly. Keep asking yourself, "does it give me that empowered, confident, delicious feeling?"

Holding onto any one item for longer than a few seconds is an indication that it's time to reconnect to the feeling. This is why you want to have the shirt that summons that feeling right next to you. When this happens, hold your happy shirt again and recharge your emotion. Hold it and remind yourself of the feeling, and then put the shirt in question in pile two.

Another indication of a need to reconnect to the authentic feeling is if you find yourself suddenly thinking everything is giving you the feeling. Doing this is only re-igniting your habit of keeping things and you're only fooling yourself.

When you do this, you are not solving any problems because you're not making decisions, you're just tricking yourself into keeping stuff. There is always a little bit of anxiety caused when we let go of things.

Once you have defined all the shirts that give you good feelings, start putting them back into the closet and drawers by hanging or folding them.

Now, let's look at the other stuff and get into that second pile. As you move further through the not-so-happy pile, create four new piles. I label these piles as: functional, donate, trash, and memorabilia.

Here is an example: if you wear a specific tank top under a lot of shirts, that would be considered functional. If you haven't worn a sweater in a while but your mother-in-law gave it to you and you can't through it away, that would be considered memorabilia.

Nine times out of ten, what you're going to pull out of that pile is memorabilia. But it must be recognized and categorized as memorabilia. Memorabilia has feelings attached to it, but this doesn't mean each item gives the same kind of happy feeling. This is why we leave memorabilia out, because even though we're working on clothes now, memorabilia will be the last thing we tackle. It's really important to go through each and every category with a fine-tooth comb. Follow this process for pants, pajamas, bras, socks, shoes, everything.

This process of sorting through and breaking this pile into four categories requires you to make a decision based on whether or not the item serves you. If you only wore a top once, it doesn't make you feel happy and otherwise does not hold value for you, or serve you, it will hold value for someone else. In this case, consign or donate it. Or, if it's in too poor a shape to donate and you're ready to let go, trash it. Don't wear it around your house to clean. Don't use it as a night shirt, or a workout shirt. We both know that you deserve to feel and look good when you are cleaning and when you are going to sleep. If you believe in recycling, you can also repurpose it by cutting it up to use as cleaning rags. If you do this, do so immediately, in the moment you're sorting, and move it to where you keep other cleaning rags. What's important is that you make an on-the-spot decision and stick to it: no takebacks.

Feeling reluctant to get rid of things you've had for years is normal. Remember, we're here to reconnect and empower ourselves to be something greater than our piles of clutter. Whenever my kids are on the fence about purging their rooms and throwing out their things,

I always ask them if they'd rather clean up things they don't use or have less stuff and be able to have more free time to make memories.

The key here is to be firm and decisive with every detail you have control over but don't confuse it with being over-controlling. By showing your spouse and children how decisive and confident you are in action, you are encouraging them to also be decisive and confident when it comes to trimming the fat out from their belongings.

Purging By Category

When purging, I highly recommend doing one category at a time. Remember, it's not just about getting rid of stuff. This is an exercise in decisiveness. Do not take that for granted. Being confrontational, even if it's with your own closet, can be mentally exhausting. My recommendation is not to work for any longer than three hours at a time because usually around the three-hour mark, you will begin to feel a decrease in energy or desire to finish. Four hours would be the absolute maximum to wrap up a project.

Paperwork Purge

I was helping a client, Joanne, purge paperwork from her home office and believe me when I tell you, there was *a lot* of paperwork. Long story short: when we left that day, we took all the paperwork with us to shred. Saying that, Joanne made the decisions on everything.

When we returned a week later, Joanne admitted that she cried when we left because she had thrown out so much. It triggered anxious feelings in her because she was letting go of paperwork that she was worried she might possibly need.

Still, the sun came up the next day and nothing happened. The following day came, and nothing happened. On the third day, Joanne realized it was okay that we got rid of all that stuff because nothing terrible happened as a result.

Paperwork tends to be one of those problem categories that sneaks up because it's a daily gradual accumulation. Once you get to a point where you have more than a little pile, you just don't want to confront it. It's too intimidating to make decisions on and the process is stressful.

There's a general statistic that we actually don't need eighty-six percent of the paperwork we have in our homes: we're just holding onto it.

When I help people declutter paperwork, I have a simple system: file, execute, or trash. Every document, every envelope, every sticky note, every piece of paper can fit into one of those categories. We're also going to break it down a little bit more. Once you've identified things you have to file, things you have to execute on, things you have to trash, you break it down again revisiting the items in the File pile and digging deeper to decide what **must** be filed and what you can actually do without.

> When deciding what to keep and toss, ask yourself two questions:
>
> 1) What happens to me if I don't have this paper? Do I get arrested? Do I get fined? Does the Bourne Identity happen?
>
> 2) If something happened tomorrow and I no longer had that piece of paper and the worst-case scenario happened, can I obtain the paper again?

Not that I'm recommending you discard it, but even your birth certificate, if it were gone, guess what? You could replace it. It would be a pain, but it is not gone forever. And that is the worst-case scenario.

Paperwork: Keep or Trash Quick Tips

Here's a quick list of paperwork that belongs safely tucked away in a small file drawer or firesafe box:

Keep Indefinitely

- Birth/Death Certificates
- Social Security Cards
- Military Discharge Papers
- Active Court Orders
- Will/Estate planning documents

What About Tax Paperwork?

In general, the longest you need to hold onto your tax records (filings and other supporting documents) is seven years after filing. This means keeping only what you or your accountant used to file your accountant used to file your taxes, which should already be in the same file. Unused receipts can be tossed. Even if you are missing a receipt, a copy can be obtained if it was paid via credit, debit or check.

Keep for 30 days in Budget Binder

- Most updated financial documents (bank statements/investment statements)
- Bills
- Receipts (for duration of return policy)

After this, once reconciled, everything else can go.

Paperwork and Storage

The way I see it, (and as I said before in the finance chapter) if you don't have a home-based business, there is absolutely no reason to have a file cabinet in your house. You can have a binder with your budget items in it and a firesafe lock-box for the important documents, like passports, wills, and other vital documents.

Bank statements are cumulative which means once you have the most recent one, the rest are void. The same goes for your bills.

While technology has taken over and many of us have moved to electronic statements and billing, you may be among those who prefer to hold on to your paper statements. The rules apply equally to both scenarios: Only keep the most recent statement as it will always be the most accurate one. If by chance you need to recover documents because you are being audited from seven years ago, your banking establishment will have an accessible digital record. Nothing bad will happen to you. I also encourage you to trash your "digital paperwork" just as often as you would trash actual papers.

Always keep the most recent store receipts only until their return policies have expired. If you think your item may break and you'll need a record of the purchase, chances are you have a transaction record on your credit card statement (or bank statement if you used your debit card) that can still be obtained. No matter what, I encourage you to consider over and over again, "What is the worst thing that will happen if I don't have that document handy?" After that, the other thing to keep in mind is if the worst-case scenario plays out can you obtain that document again?

Warranties usually require that you register them online and therefore, there is record of them. Appliance manuals can usually be found online, or you can safely tape them to the back of the larger corresponding appliances.

A good exercise after realizing what exactly you need or don't when it comes to paperwork is this: The next time you get your mail, use the time it takes to walk from the mailbox to the front door to sort following the execute, trash, file approach. Eliminate the junk mail immediately (keep in mind, you can also affix a friendly note to your mailbox asking for no flyers and junk mail). However, if you receive junk mail, by throwing it into the recycling immediately upon receiving it, you're already eliminating fifty to sixty percent of the paperwork that comes into your house before you can reach your front door. You're making a decision in the moment. Do this a few more times and suddenly it's not an overwhelming part of the process, it's a daily habit. Because you are exercising this skill, you'll be able to make decisions a little faster and a little more confidently not only in your home but in other aspects of your life.

What about coupons, you ask? If you are still collecting paper coupons, keep an envelope in your purse with the coupons that you would like to use. If you don't use them by the time they expire, toss them. This way at least they have a place and you can keep the quantity under control. Also, you will never have to go back home for the coupon because it's already with you. If you always have your smartphone with you and you're keen to leverage technology, consider looking into one of the many coupon and savings apps out there and cut out the extraneous paper entirely.

There are all kinds of envelopes you may receive from friends and family that have a return address on them that you don't want to lose. What I do in this case is create a spreadsheet in Excel on which I put everyone's addresses. From here, this can easily be uploaded into address book software or used to mail merge into Word so your holiday card envelopes can be printed simply and quickly.

As with anything that feels overwhelming, start with tossing something small, like the envelope the bill came in. This small act is the first step to disrupting your habit of keeping papers. Remember, you are retraining your brain to let go of things that gave you emotional security. Stay patient with yourself but keep moving forward. Eventually, you will become comfortable with the fact that nothing will happen when you throw that little piece of paper away.

Memorabilia

Shining a light on the fact that most people have so much memorabilia makes you see just how much crazy logic can take hold of even the most minimal minds. This is best explained through my own personal example with regards to my kids.

I remember when Vanessa (my oldest) was a toddler and she drew her first line on a piece of paper. I celebrated my baby drawing her first line and was so excited about it. In the moment, I had an emotional attachment to that paper.

Ten years, three more kids, and dozens of lines later I come across what might have been that line. There's no name on it, and no emotional attachment. I don't have anxiety over not having it anymore.

Working with memorabilia, we apply the same logic as we did when we pulled out that first shirt that ignited a good feeling in you. When you put all of your memorabilia all across the table—and I'm talking shirts, photos, jewelry, handwritten notes—you have a clear perspective of all of your memorabilia all at once and you can decide what is the most memorable to you. What things do you hold the dearest?

The only difference between that piece of paper I wanted so much to keep ten years ago and the same piece of paper rediscovered recently, is my emotional connection to it. That's it. Dealing with emotions is all part of the process when you're sorting and purging. Get all that memorabilia in its rightful place so it can be categorized and dealt with properly. You will find your decisiveness start to mature after about three sessions.

The first session will be like pulling teeth. Nobody wants to let anything go. But once you take it all out of the house, you realize that nothing bad is going to happen. The second session gets a little bit easier, and by the third session you'll find you are refining your decision-making skills.

After the purge is complete for a category, act on those piles as quickly as possible. Donate, trash, and put the memorabilia with other memorabilia all on the same day otherwise the process will not work. After you've gone through the process three times, you'll notice how much easier it is to make decisions and let that clutter go. Also, after three sessions, you are now equipped to coach the rest of your family.

Everyone Else's Stuff

While it may fall to you to purge the paperwork and manage the memorabilia, it is not your responsibility to purge your spouse's or your kids' belongings.

You may be thinking:

1. There's no way they're going to do that.
2. There's no way they're going to do it right.

Well, let go, momma. Because they are going to do it (with your coaching) and they are not going to keep all the dresses, ties, and shirts that you like. In fact, you may cringe at all the things they pick. But guess what? Their wardrobe is not up to you. By letting them do it themselves, with your support, you are showing them that you respect them and their thoughts and ideas, and you value them as individuals.

The result? A house full of happier human beings.

Take a moment and think about how you would feel if someone picked out your clothes daily or told you how to keep your room. You wouldn't feel so good about yourself and the constant critique you're undergoing, would you?

That said, we still have words of guidance and encouragement. For example, I won't tell my kids to clean their bedrooms. What I do tell them is that it's okay if they like a messy room, but that's not my preference. If they want me to come into their room, it must be tidy.

I wish I had a recording of the first time we were about to be late to baseball and my son asked me for help finding his socks. When I saw the state of his room, I said, "Sorry! I can't come in here. Mom's allergic to this mess." The look on his face was priceless! We were late to practice that day and he was really upset.

Later, when I asked him why he was upset, he replied that he was disappointed in himself for not being prepared. Had I not asked him, I definitely would have assumed that he was upset with me. But instead of feeling the "mom-guilt" we tend to put on ourselves, I was proud of him. He took ownership of his decisions. Don't get me wrong, he doesn't keep his room immaculate all the time, but he tries, and he knows that when he doesn't, he often dislikes the outcome.

The other stipulation I have is company, friends included. The kids have an understanding that when a room is messy, it's much easier to trip or get hurt or have an accident. They understand that if they want a friend over, we must provide a safe environment.

Helping kids sort their toys, whether in their rooms or in the communal play room, is another great area for kids to learn decision-making. Let the kids decide for themselves. Sit with them and encourage them to make two piles: toys they want and toys they can live without. If they're having trouble letting go, have them imagine they're stuck on a tiny island (in this case, a box that is 12 cubic inches), and ask them what they'd take to the island. Whatever they don't bring, they can live without.

By highlighting and talking about each item in the box, they're highlighting the importance of the items that made the cut, and conversely the reasons why the other items didn't, which will help lay the foundations for effective and prompt decision-making in their future.

Keeping Holiday Clutter To A Minimum

In our household we also do a pre-Christmas purge, and use this tiny island analogy again here. When it comes to the decor, organizing and storing properly helps your holiday spirit items last longer. From there, it can be a slow build.

When my husband and I celebrated our first Christmas together, we didn't have enough money to buy the type of ornaments we liked. Instead, we purchased only one for each person in our household. Every year since then, each person gets one new ornament. Our tree is getting so full that even the side against the wall gets ornaments, too.

The tips I'm sharing about sorting and purging are quite general here, because it's really all about making decisions. In my household, as a way of keeping the clutter under control for other holidays and celebrations, I avoid purchasing themed party supplies that can be pricey and rarely get used twice because they quickly go out of style. Instead of themed decor, I keep a stock of generic birthday party items on hand at all times.

I believe in celebrations of all kinds, from holidays to birthday parties. I don't care about the age. I don't care if it's a half birthday. I don't care if it's somebody else's birthday. I like being ready to throw a party at a moment's notice. For that reason, I keep some staples on hand:

1. Streamers (every color—accumulate over time)
2. Balloons (Same as 1.)
3. Colorful paper plates (Same as 1.)
4. Rolls of colorful tablecloth (basic colors that can match anything)
5. A shimmer curtain (basic color)
6. Cardstock for printing invitations, menus, and customizable themed decor.

With these items, you can throw a party in about an hour without being excessive or breaking the bank.

These items are part of my curated box of party supplies that I know I will absolutely use. I keep it contained to a storage cart that is about two feet by three feet and simply fill it with our kids' favorite colors (buy the largest size because the price per unit is cheaper) and replace as necessary—usually once every three years or so.

Then, I tuck away all of the generic party items in one side of the garage and place the solid colored table cloth rolls neatly behind it (in between the cart and the wall). I don't go overboard with additional themed purchases, I just replace colors as needed.

Keep in mind, decluttering is about purging what does not bring you happiness and what is not useful. If you are bulk buying carefully curated items that will be used time and time again (like in our household which has six birthdays a year) that is having great insight—which is step two of my 3-step methodology. We'll discuss insightfulness –and start applying it in practice—in the next chapter.

Now, that wasn't so bad, was it? By feeling your way through your belongings and really connecting with what gives you good feelings and what doesn't, you too can start to declutter your home. There is no right or wrong, and what is most important is that you set yourself up for success. If this makes you incredibly anxious and your palms are sweating as you read the chapter, know that there are tons of coaches and businesses out there happy to support you and do this with you. Chances are, you've got an in-house sort-and-purger already amongst your own kids, and they may love helping in this area!

Keep in mind, if you did any of this – even just a moment of paperwork sorting—then you've already begun dipping into the real skill at play here: decisiveness.

Use these tips, start being decisive and tackle the clutter so you can spend your time and energy on what matters most: taking care of yourself and doing the things you love, like hanging out with your kids and your sweetie, making memories and fulfilling your own passions.

⇆ Feedback from the Team

Here's what one of my kids had to say when I asked: How do you feel when you get rid of your stuff?

"I used to be sad about it, but now I don't really care if I don't use it that much anymore. If, like, I'm not using something another kid could. Except penguin, I'm never getting rid of penguin."

9:

Prioritize to Organize

Following the sort and purge, we move into organizing. This is the last step before systemizing the chore responsibilities.

Organizing is nothing more than assigning useful items a home. It does, however, require some insight, or the second step of our 3-step methodology.

Please know this: you are already insightful. It is likely that your things are already in the right room, possibly even in the right place. To have insight is to make the connection between your things and when, where, and how they are being used. For example, keeping the wooden spoons on the counter beside the stove where you cook is insightful. As opposed to keeping them in some bottom drawer where you would have to step away from your bubbling tomato sauce, walk over to the drawer, and dig through it to find the spoon. By the time you come back, the sauce would be burning on the bottom of the pot! Using your insight is what helps avoid this kind of organizational mayhem.

The practice of applying insight to your organizing is all about fine-tuning a skill you already possess. By using insight, you are now going to put a magnifying glass to the frequency of usage for each item you are going to put away.

At the end of the day, organization is simply about giving useful items a home in the most appropriate place.

In many ways, the hard work is over once you've made the tough decisions and sorted what's being used from what's not. Track the amount of times you use something—along with where, when and how you use it—and use this data to determine where the item is best placed. By evaluating and predicting your usage you will develop a clear understanding for why items should be stored in specific places. Cultivating this understanding is what it means to be insightful.

Everything Needs a Home

When teaching my kids about organization, I asked them how they would feel if they didn't know where their home was, or if it moved often? Imagine how silly that would be. Walking into a different neighbor's house every night because you don't know where you live. That's how your toys, electronics, and clothes feel.

You may think for a moment how silly that is, personi-fying material objects. But is it any sillier than attaching a feeling to an object? Think back for a moment to when you couldn't let that top go that your significant other bought you on your honeymoon. Whether you admit it or not, you assigned an emotional attachment to an object that at the end of the day is nothing more than an object. Prac-tice makes perfect and the more you practice recognizing emotions, the more emotionally mature you will become.

Creating Efficient Work Flow

Now that you have sorted and purged, it's time to take what remains and put it in the most appropriate place for maximum functionality. Your unique organizing template begins with an assessment of your individual work flow.

There are some obvious things you can implement as you begin improving your workflow, like using baskets to organize "catch-all" areas: under kitchen/bathroom sinks, junk drawers, nightstands, or adding compart-ments to drawers to allow miscellaneous items to be more easily organized.

The follow-up piece is really the most important here: Is your home set-up to fit your work flow?

I often use the example of clothes on the floor. I must have had the "talk" with my husband a hundred times about those damn socks on the floor. I couldn't under-stand for the life of me what was so hard about picking them up and putting them into the hamper.

I finally gave up. As a joke, in a moment of waving the white flag, I moved the hamper to the exact spot that those darn socks kept landing. My husband didn't even realize that I was being sarcastic. Still, I placed the hamper tucked away near that spot, and poof, the problem was gone.

That's when I realized that I was being unfair to my family. I had been putting design over function when I actually could have had both.

So, I did my own work flow assessment. I thought of all the places I had asked people to put things away and kept this present in my mind as I moved from room to room. I put a basket in the bathroom for the toothbrushes. The Q-tips had a decorative holder. The bread had a basket. The make-up had a decorative box that fit on the counter top. The shoes had a chest.

Once I reconfigured the spaces and put organizational storage in places where it was missing, the house was no longer working against our natural flow of living. The systems were in place. Only after your systems are in place is it fair to hold your team accountable for their daily responsibilities.

This step of organizing is also intended to help with the ongoing accumulation of clutter. You may have to do one big sort and purge to kick off the whole process, but if you are committed to organizing and staying organized, as well as making organization a natural extension of the work flow in your house, then you're only setting yourself up for success in the fight against ongoing clutter. Because we are always accumulating, that is one guarantee. We must purge as often and as consistently as we accumulate. By staying on top of your organization, you will save time in the long-run and manage the accumulation of stuff on an ongoing basis.

↹ Feedback From The Team

Here's what one of my children had to say when I asked them:

What was a problem area for you to keep tidy? How did you fix it?

"We fixed it by moving the room around a lot. First of all, we changed where the dresser was and then I re-folded my clothes and cleaned off my entire dresser and also, I didn't keep everything. A lot of it, well actually not a lot of it but I did throw most of it out. Because it was getting kinda messy and my bottom drawer was just full. Usually when we are getting rid of stuff. 'If you don't love it, don't keep it.' A lot of the stuff that I threw out was just a whole bunch of junk, I really didn't need it. And then I reorganized it and I just finished it up."

10:

Managing the Team: Department Of Janitorial and Sanitation

Now we can really start having fun. It's time to talk about chores! When it comes to chores, we will draw on a lot of things, not least of which is the third step in our 3-step methodology: consistency. Not only do I wish to help you set up a chore system that works for you and your family, but a system wherein everyone can remain consistent. Consistency, you'll find, is key when it comes to getting chores done.

This is the real test of your management and team-building skills. This is the Janitorial Department, Department of Sanitation and Cleanliness. Is your team the kind that vanish when you pull out the chore list? Or do you all do chores with gusto after trying a new system, only to be inconsistent thereafter? Are you ready to learn a new approach, one that truly divides the chores between all the team members that make up your family and allows for chores to be done consistently—and with no nagging? If so, this chapter is for you!

Relinquish Control

Before we get into the nitty-gritty of chores and systems, I would like to speak to the element of control. There have already likely been times in this book when you were reading and thinking "I could never give up control of that!" Well, if you really want to rock it as a great Chief Executive Mom, you have to get a handle on control. And I find especially with chores that it's easy to get caught up in wanting to control everything and everyone. But that's not helpful—for you or your family.

The way I see it, control is constantly holding others accountable to your expectations and not allowing others to set their own. Control can also look like assuming someone else can read your mind and effectively accomplish something to your standards and expectations. Thus when it comes time to take care of the chores, get the kids ready for school, do homework, cook dinner, etc... if we allow ourselves to get angry or disappointed by the outcome of someone else executing those tasks, it's simply because we're not giving them the respect they deserve by allowing them to set their own standards and continue to raise their own bar.

You're only the sum of your own experiences, so if you've had more experience than your teenager or husband when it comes to cooking, for example, obviously your standard and your expectation of the meal is going to be much different than theirs. But if you allow another member of the household to take control of their responsibilities in their own way, then they have the opportunity to gain experience. They come into your family like an entry-level employee joins a corporation, gaining experience and setting their own standard with the help of some positive critical feedback. The person that's empowered to carry out their responsibility should be setting their own expectations. With coaching and continuous feedback, we troubleshoot and make them better at their job and, more importantly, encourage their passion and excitement because when they love what they're doing they're going to want to get better at it.

With all this in mind, use the tips and systems to help build a new chore structure. By letting go of control and allowing everyone to participate based on their experience you are ultimately creating the best feeling of ownership in everyone. When the team feels they're contributing, they are eager to help—even if that means doing chores.

Implementing a New Chore System

There are two initial strategies to consider when you start implementing a new chore system:

1. Assign chores to each individual's strengths.

2. Break down each room that needs to be covered into three levels: Insides, Outsides, and Invisibles. Those will be your primary components.

"Insides" refers to the details behind closed doors, like inside dresser drawers, inside cabinets, closets, and pantries.

"Outsides" is exactly what it sounds like: does the room look tidy? Are the things put properly in their homes? Are the dishes clean? Are the clothes put away? Are the beds made? While this statement means something different in every room, it doesn't mean a different person is assigned to different components.

"Invisibles" refers to disinfecting: wiping down countertops, windows, and floors. Getting rid of the invisible germs.

When assigning chores, take into consideration that each room's cleaning team and roles may look different. For example, if we are talking about Lucy's bedroom, she'll be in charge of "Insides" and "Outsides": dresser drawers, closets, chests. It just doesn't make sense to have someone else putting her stuff away and keeping the insides tidy. Because these are her personal belongings, she is the most capable person to own those jobs.

However, in a shared place like the kitchen, it may make sense to have one person assigned to outsides, another person assigned to insides, and a third person assigned to invisibles because it's such a big job and a commonly used room. That room likely requires the most frequent attention in all three of your primary components. One person might take care of rinsing dishes and loading the dishwasher, another might put the clean dishes away, and the third person would wipe down the surfaces. Doing it this way allows the family to work as a team with small responsibilities.

Address your household duties keeping those points in mind, assign and breakdown, and then divvy up the duties amongst each person in the family.

After this is done, assign a shift. Any house that is lived in will require constant upkeep but allowing the upkeep of the house to control your whole day is ludicrous. I hear many parents tell their kids they can't play until their chores are done. These same parents will likely complain that getting their kid to do the chores is a struggle and really believe taking play time away is the only way for the kids to get their chores done.

Consider this instead: you may have a communication issue with your kid if you are continuously barking at them to do chores and negotiating favorite things. If that's what is going on, it means that they are not buying into your processes. They are resisting because they have no reason to believe in what you are asking of them. They haven't yet learned that a tidy house is a peaceful house, a place where they can find their baseball glove whenever they want it. In a tidy house there is less possibility for dust mites and viruses which means less time being sick and more time playing with their friends. If the house is maintained a solid eighty percent of the time, that also means you'll say yes to more things. Can we play chess? Yes! (Instead of, "Let's put the last game away first.") Can I have a snack? Yes! (Instead of, "Hold on, I'm doing the dishes.") Can I have a friend over? Yes! (Instead of, "Only if your room is clean.") More yes!

Creating Your Weekly Chore System

The timing of each chore shift matters. If you pile chores onto the end of everyone's day, you don't take into consideration how long or difficult everyone's day might have been. I mean, you remember what it was like in school? The work, the drama, the constant struggle to fit in. It's exhausting. A little respect there would go a really long way.

Instead, this is what I recommend. Contingent on schedule of course, initiate an AM checklist and a PM checklist. Yes, I know getting out the door is hard enough, but trust me on this one...and don't give up.

This suggestion is basically to split a big chore list into smaller increments to be done in the morning, around noon, and in the evening. It may take a little getting used to but over time you will see this approach yields quicker and more consistent results. Again, this system is about breaking down weekly chores and using incremental time, and shorter spurts of time, to get them done.

Sample Chore Schedule

1. The AM Chores (to be complete by 9 a.m.)
   - Wash dirty laundry

- Put away clean laundry
- Empty trash cans
- Make beds.

2. (Outside of school days) (to be done between 11 a.m. and 2 p.m.)
   - Dry laundry
   - Wash dishes
   - Wipe down surfaces

3. PM (to be done between 8-10 p.m., with attention to running the vacuum before people go to bed)
   - Fold laundry
   - Vacuum
   - Wash dishes

Morning chores might be the hardest to start implementing, so start slowly on the first day by working in whatever you can along with getting ready for the day. If you and your family can't get it all done (and it's okay, it doesn't matter how much you can't get done), simply set the alarms to go five minutes earlier the next day—and only five minutes earlier. We don't want to be dramatic about it. There is no need for yelling or anything like that! Just try your best and allow your family to try their best, then get up five minutes earlier the next day. Five minutes is completely reasonable, you will not be the bad guy and it won't be that much harder for them to get out of bed. But if they know that you'll add five minutes a day, I guarantee they will get it done.

Accountability is key here. Have your checklists printed as handouts and put them on the fridge or taped to a wall in your kids' rooms. You might even like to use an app (our family likes Habitica). Take a moment every single morning to move through that checklist with them and make sure it is done.

It hoefully goes without saying that you have to change your behavior, too. The morning list truly is the most difficult to get through but believe me the effects of this will ripple into everyone's day. I would even go so far as to say your kids' school work may improve. Much like the now-famous Naval Admiral William McRaven's viral speech about why it's essential to make our beds each day, these are the small things we do in our lives that build our character. If we practice accountability daily, your kids will get into the habit of being accountable consistently.

Tools for Systematizing Your Chores

Here are some tools you may find useful to help effectively carry out this section:

- A room-by-room scorecard breakdown
- A master chore list (every line item)
- Schedule
- Assignment sheet - AM version/ noon version (when applicable) /PM version

  As we just discussed, split your master chore list into smaller increments in the morning, noon, and evening for quicker, more consistent results. Here is the example I shared earlier, once more:

  i. AM (9 a.m. deadline): Wash dirty laundry/put away clean laundry, empty trash cans, make beds.
  ii. Noon (11 a.m.-2 p.m.): Dry laundry, wash dishes, wipe down surfaces.
  iii. PM (8-10 p.m.): Fold laundry, vacuum, wash dishes.
- An accountability tracker - this is a long-term tracking sheet.
- Rewards program (if applicable)
- Rotation Schedule (if applicable)

On Rewards

Let's talk for a moment about a rewards program. I'm pretty straight to the point, so our family deals in allowances, which I discussed in the Finance chapter. In short, instead of incentivizing with rewards, per se, they are incentivized by our allowance system.

I like this system mostly because it's a mini version of adult life. It gives the kids a sense of working to get by and working hard to make your goals. I also like that I never had trouble teaching them percentages. It's relevant so it sticks. And the best part: I never feel like I have to say yes or no at the store. They work hard to make their own money and they can spend it however they would like. I don't buy for anyone unless it's their birthday or a holiday. Some people may think that's mean-mommy-ing, but because they buy their own things, they take better care of those things and they truly come full circle, buying into why it's important to keep things in order.

In a system like this, you are less of a controlling bad guy. You have an accountability system in place. They get paid and they work toward what they want. Win. Win. Win.

Making Chores Less Of A Chore

You deserve to live in a home that is struggle-free when it comes to getting chores done, and where you don't do them all by yourself. Give these systems a try! Just ensure you and your team have completed the sorting, purging, and organizing before you begin to implement your new chore routine.

As we talked about in chapter 3, getting the family on board whenever you make a change can be a bit bumpy. Use the tools you have and try not to cave into old habits (like bribes or yelling). The work will get done. Your kids will benefit by helping out, and your partner is more than capable of participating and backing you up.

Chores can bring out the best or the worst in households; use your skills, the tips I've shared, and your ability to create a team out of your family to make doing chores less of a, for lack of a better word, chore!

⇆ Feedback From The Team

Here's what my kids had to say when I asked them a few questions.

What's your favorite responsibility?
"Taking care of penguin."

What are some grown-up things that you do in the house?

1. *Clean the table*
2. *Clean family room*
3. *Clean credenza*
4. *Playing pool*
5. *Cooking*

You have a lot of responsibility. How does that make you feel?

"It can be a little overwhelming, but it makes me feel mature. It makes me feel older and it makes me feel good because you guys trust me with things and you give me the privilege to have my own responsibility— sometimes they're big, sometimes, they're small, sometimes they're perfect."

Do you feel that our household is fair?

"Sometimes I'm just in the moment and after we talk it through I think that most kids might have it worse. And then I realize that whatever I have to do is not so bad."

Are your chores hard?

No

Did they used to be hard?

Yeah, kinda

Why aren't they hard anymore?

I've gotten used to them. I've gotten quicker cleaning them.

Do you mind doing chores?

No.

Why not?

Well, I also get exercise while I'm cleaning.

11:

Human Resources &
Personal Development
(aka extracurricular
Activities)

When I first became a mom, I read every book and article I could get my hands on so I could raise the "perfect" kid. And Vanessa was. We did time-out the way the book said, we communicated on the same level, we said exactly what we meant and meant exactly what we said. She listened like an angel.

Then Jacob came along, and I was able to keep up with exactly half of what I practiced the first time around. When he cried, he cried a little longer. When Vanessa asked for something, her wait time was extended. It was no longer about either one of them because it was about both of them.

Lucy came along next, and time and practices were split yet again. By the time Nora came, it was like the Wild West. I fully acknowledge that everyone's threshold for Wild West status varies, mine was four. I have some mom friends that achieved that status at two and some that achieved at six. In fact, I'll often say I knew two was my cut-off after I had three.

I noticed as they grew though, that Vanessa, my oldest, the one whom I gave the most attention to, was the best behaved and the most responsible. At the same time, she also had the most stress triggers and was the most dependent. In drastic contrast, Nora, my youngest, who was the most "neglected" (to use the term loosely) was the happiest and most independent. Jacob and Lucy, in the middle, were varying degrees in between. Vanessa and Jacob are most likely to ask for permission while Lucy and Nora are prone to asking for forgiveness.

As a parent, my main objective is to outline multiple paths and to be the wheels of their car. By this I mean, I want to *support* them but not *steer* them.

Though it seems like Vanessa is the "best behaved" kid, Vanessa also relies on me the most to do the driving. She questions her decisions rather than living through the experiences and learning. When it comes to basic survival skills, like preparing food, she'll consider all her options, ask my opinion, and even delay making a decision in hopes of being guided, whereas the others will at least try something. Don't get me wrong, I am by no means insulting her character. I am questioning whether I have given her enough support so that she is confident enough to act on her decisions without my blessing because it is inevitable that I will not be around forever. All any mother wants is for her children to be happy and successful. But those two terms need to be defined by the child. This is why exposing your kids to extracurricular activities and letting them choose their experiences is so helpful; it becomes part of what allows them to define those terms.

When my kids hit three to four years old, we started getting involved in soccer, dance, baseball, and acrobatics. I wanted to commit to these extra activities at an early age so that when my kids got older, if they wanted to continue, they already had years of skill under their belts. I often found myself rushing around, getting them to where they had to be. Finding the ballet slippers and tap shoes, finding the baseball mitts and cleats. And oh, God, why did we always lose the hat on picture day?!

Eventually, I had enough. We had the calendar, the kids knew how to read it and they knew how to tell time. Toward the end of their year, I stopped reminding them. I stopped the pressure. We had the talk about how they will make it a priority if they really want to do something, only to miss two classes their first week.

What kind of lesson did I teach them? Maybe it was a lesson they taught me. I learned what my kids were actually interested in. I learned that when I did not sign them up for next year's dance team, they didn't care. I learned that my daughter preferred chin guards over leg warmers and was a beast on the soccer field.

I learned my son really was invested in his baseball team as he stood at the door five minutes early waiting on me.

I also learned that happy people don't need to be micromanaged. Achieving happiness requires investing in yourself—and this goes for kids, too. When your kid has a vested interest in what they are doing, they take ownership of it and all of its components. The gear, the schedule, the commute, the efforts in practicing, the commitment, the result. And most importantly, they are making the best decisions for themselves. Knowing the feeling of what makes you happy will help be your compass. Action equals happiness, whereas inaction is an indication of uninterest.

Let The Kids Control Their Schedule

Your kids' minds may be blown the first time they are given control of their own schedule. We have a couple of rules in our household to help keep the schedule from being overwhelming:

1. Each kid finishes what they start.
2. Everyone in the family gets equal parts of the schedule (this mitigates kids picking six extracurriculars over the next ten weeks).
3. Don't say no to extra activity requests, just map them out on the calendar for next season so your kid has something to look forward to.

In addition to learning how to choose what they like, your kid is also learning about their pace. Everyone has their own limits on overstimulation and your kid is no different. You may have one child that can be booked every minute of the day and still have mental energy, while your other child really enjoys a day to themselves to think and explore their imagination. Imagination looks different at every age and never goes away.

That could be a great gauge to help guide your children as well. It's possible your kid will think they need to be scheduled every minute of the day because they have otherwise never experienced a day with their thoughts. That is one of the dangers of over-scheduling. Too much stimulation doesn't leave room for imagination.

Leave Room For Imagination

You'd be surprised at what your kid will think of when they have time to themselves. My very first experience with this stemmed from a punishment. A child of mine who shall not be named used a wrong word in a right way. I knew he was testing his boundaries and didn't want to overreact (whoops—now you know who it is, given I only have one son!) His punishment was to have a day in his room to think about that word, his feelings, and what other words he could've used to express himself. No electronics—just his thoughts.

At the end of the day, not only did he apologize, but he taught himself how to play a song on his guitar—an instrument he didn't even know how to play before that day! While he was sorry for his behavior the day before, he expressed his gratitude for having had a day to himself just to think and have some quiet time. At only eight years old, he had begun to understand the importance of attuning to his own pace. Now, he is more easily able to identify when he is overstimulated. Even though it's not consistent, or there are times when he doesn't want to step away from the crowd, both of us can identify when he's ready for some down time, and he understands and appreciates that awareness.

As your kids attune to themselves and start to be held accountable for their interests and their commitment to the extracurricular activities they've chosen, you will watch as they blossom into their unique selves. You'll see interests bloom. As a parent, I want my kids to experience lots of things as they feel into who they are and what they like.

That said, I do keep an eye on perfectionist tendencies or tendencies towards comparing with others.

Keep Perfectionism At Bay

"My kid is a perfectionist," is something I hear parents say a lot these days. As a parent of one myself, I know how good it feels to brag. But as an educator, I admit that I worry as much about Vanessa's education as I do Jacob's (for whom sitting down to focus can be a challenge). That said, Jacob is a gifted athlete. Perfectionism, however, is often unnoticed, and usually very positively construed in the world. I was worried that if Vanessa was giving in to perfectionist tendencies too much, that her education would suffer because she wasn't being challenged enough.

To avoid the pitfalls of perfectionism, I came up with the following reminders, which I share with my kids whenever necessary:

- Learning isn't about getting the answers right, it's about being challenged and learning how to overcome said challenge.
- Mistakes should be expected, not feared. Jacob knows he's not always going to knock the ball out of the park. But because it's assumed, it's never a crushing disappointment when it doesn't happen.
- As parents, we have to change our tune. Instead of saying, "You're so smart," we prefer, "I noticed you worked really hard on that." Again, if my son has a bad day on the field, he isn't beating himself up for not being athletic enough, he simply knows it is time to hit the batting cage.

It is terribly easy to be proud parents. The real challenge is in accepting that sometimes our kids need a little more than empty accolades to make them better students, and in turn, better people.

Extracurricular activities are paramount to your child's personal development, and letting them really engage with the entire process, from choosing the activity to planning, scheduling, and even getting themselves to practice wherever possible, makes them own their participation in an invested way. It's truly one of the joys of motherhood to watch our children blossom into their unique personalities, find things they love doing, and seek to grow within that activity. Don't forget, your kids are also watching you, so by modeling your new approach to life (hint: chapter 3!) you are also showing them that being a lifelong learner is an abundant way to live!

↳ Feedback from the Team

Here is how one of my kids responded when I asked: How do you feel about being in control of your own schedule?

"Having someone control your routine can be stressful. You have someone telling you what to do and how to do it all the time. You probably would like to be free and make your own decisions. Since I'm not an adult yet, I still have limitations. Like I explained this before, being in control is like a house. An apartment would be someone controlling you and your daily routine all the time. A house is more spacious and you have more room to run around and be free. A mansion would be you, completely free, but since I'm not an adult yet, I can't be in the mansion. You have to have a certain amount of responsibility to live in the mansion; to live in a world where you make all of your own decisions."

12:

The Sweet Spot

With a lifestyle as busy as your family's it can be incredibly difficult to manage a healthy diet. The key to keeping a family healthy via nutrition is buy-in, and not just your kids' or your spouse's, but your own especially. There are several ways to achieve a healthy lifestyle.

I do want to preface this section with this: I am no doctor and will not speak to any specific ailments or results. My thoughts on this are based on my own practices and I recommend seeing a health care provider for any particular health issues you may have.

Healthy Mama, Healthy Family

I have come to believe that when it comes to health, what we consume is everything. Again, everything I'm sharing is based on personal experience, not medical expertise.

That said, in my experience there is a direct correlation between what I eat and how I feel. I'm talking about everything from the level of energy I have, to how many hugs I need per day.

My current approach to health via nutrition includes starting my day with a super smoothie. Since I'm on the go every minute of the day, I need to get my nutrients in any chance I get.

This is what my smoothie generally includes:

- kale
- banana
- whole yogurt
- chia seed
- flax seed
- women's multi-vitamin
- coconut oil
- collagen
- protein powder
- glucosamine/chondroitin
- and turmeric/curcumin (if I'm feeling like I need an extra boost).

This magical elixir is not always my favorite snack (because I have one every day) but I know to keep having them because when I don't, I feel it immediately. I feel less energetic, I get hungry quicker, and I feel like something is missing. Drinking this smoothie at 6 a.m. in conjunction with a coffee around 9 a.m. keeps me plowing through until lunch time. As an added benefit, it also makes my hair as shiny as it was when I was on pre-natal vitamins.

I eat lunch usually between 1 and 2 p.m. As I describe in Chapter 7, in our household, lunch is our primary meal of the day. Whatever most people have for dinner in terms of it being the main meal is what our family has for lunch.

I recommend lunch as the big feast of the day because your body has more time to digest and you won't have to work hard at digestion during sleep. Personally, a lighter meal in the evening is my preference, as I find that the heavier and later my meal is, the more bloated I feel the next morning.

Depending on how your household has been operating, you may not feel good about buying certain foods or eating things that no one else in the family eats. While generally a family eats the same foods, obviously my kids don't want kale, collagen and turmeric in their smoothies! I do what I do to stay healthy, and this is the invitation to you.

Remembering the discussion in chapter 3, if you're not healthy, the family isn't healthy. Start listening to your body and figure out the best diet choices for you, the diet that brings you the most energy and happiness each day.

Cut The Sugar

Cutting white granulated sugar out of our diets has worked wonders for my family. We do not purchase soda under any circumstances, not for parties, not for dinners, not when the friends come over, not even when my Dad comes to town (sorry, Dad!) The closest you will get to a sweet drink in our house is homemade iced tea or lemonade—and not the powdered stuff, the real stuff. It's not pretentious. Buying soda and sugared drinks is a waste of money. These drinks also alter your taste buds.

Here are my rules about sugar in the house:

- Donuts are not breakfast! They are a snack, at best.
- Diet soda is the worst and silliest excuse for dieting, ever.
- Ice cream is *not* a source of calcium.
- Store-bought fruit juices are vessels for sugar.
- White bread has sugar in it.
- The longer the shelf life, the more crap they put in it.
- Yogurt is not supposed to have sugar in it.
- If your kid can't identify where the ingredient on the label came from, they probably shouldn't consume it.

Simply put, when it comes to food, we have to wake up. In fact, I challenge you to cut back on sugar for 15 days. Research all forms, derivatives, and cousins of sugar, and then eliminate it from your pantry, fridge, and shopping cart. I guarantee that after a couple of weeks, your taste buds will change. Real food will taste better and you will be able to taste the chemical flavor of white granulated sugar when/if the time comes that it is reintroduced.

I had terrible acne from preteen to adulthood until I eliminated white sugar. In the first two weeks after quitting, I experienced extreme exhaustion and body aches. The culprit? Sugar. Mood swings? Sugar. You get the picture.

What do you do after those two weeks are up? Explore the vast array of natural, unprocessed, sugar alternatives available. Use fresh local honey if you need to sweeten your yogurt/tea/cereal. Use cane sugar or coconut sugar if you want candy coffee. Try using home-made applesauce as a sugar substitute in your baked goods. Fresh fruit is really nature's candy.

I wouldn't recommend reintroducing sugary snacks into the household until everyone in the household can truly understand the difference between snacks and food. In addition, anytime someone is thirsty, water is the only drink that hydrates. If you or someone in your household doesn't like water, that's a sure sign they have taste buds that are not in their purest form.

Low-Sugar Kids

I definitely will tell you, however, that raising health-conscious, low-sugar children can be challenging at times. But keep in mind, all things are best done in moderation. Rather than obsessing over a cupcake at a kid's birthday party, drawing awareness to the fact that the cupcake is just a snack celebrating our friend is a more important lesson. While I don't personally agree with all the sugar that's pushed on our children through processed foods, I also don't agree with being so extreme that the kids are afraid of sugar or the issue puts a damper on their childhood. Rather than taking it away completely, we would rather our kids experience it in small doses. This way they can feel and experience what sugar does to their body, and how it affects their minds and behavior. I promise it's only a matter of time until they understand how healthy eating habits affect them positively.

Making homemade fresh-baked goods is a great way to control sugar intake. We're able to cut the sugar in recipes in half or eliminate white sugar and replace it with brown. By doing this our children have a lower tolerance for white sugar and when they finally do get around to having some, they don't care for it.

Remember, this isn't about shielding them from all things that could hurt them, it's about letting them experience things in a safe environment so they can understand outcomes and be more knowledgeable about future decisions. Any friend of mine that I knew growing up with strict parents ended up rebelling. The last thing I want is for my kids or my spouse to rebel because I'm trying to control what they put into their bodies. It's my job to educate and train them for life.

We have a practice on Halloween that has become adopted by all of our friends and their children. On Halloween night after everyone's collected candy, we all come back to the house, check the candy, sort it, and then the timer goes on. The kids have ten minutes to eat as much candy as they want and the rest of the candy goes straight to the garbage. Now you would think that eating candy for ten minutes would be a kid's dream and they sure behave like it is, but after about three minutes they all slow down and by minute seven they're usually done. By giving them the freedom to scarf down as many sweets as they want for an occasion like Halloween, it reminds them that we're embracing and honoring their childhood and feel that we have respect for their choices. We are all happy in the moment and nobody minds the day after when all the candy has gone into the trash and we're back to our healthy eating habits.

Stay Hydrated

It may sound silly, but we only drink water in our house. When I was a kid, my parents gave me juice whenever I was thirsty. As a result, when I became a young adult I confused dehydration with a craving for fruit. It wasn't until my late twenties that I trained my body to drink water every time I thought I wanted fruit. Prior to that I didn't like water at all. Now I understand when my body is thirsty.

We may take something so small as a glass of water for granted, but it really does make an impact on our children and what they take in on a daily basis.

It's not as challenging as one might think to create healthy habits for both ourselves and our families. Being consistent and role-modeling are key here; if your kids hear you say "no sugar snacks" only to see your used Snickers bar wrapper lying around, then the jig is up. Of course, you wouldn't choose to eat a Snickers bar if you prioritized your good health and approached your eating habits with integrity and commitment. The health of your family starts at the table, and as Chief Executive Mom, you have an essential responsibility to feed your family the most healthful, nutritious way possible.

↳ Feedback From The Team

Here is what one of my children say when I asked them: What is your favorite snack?

"All time favorite? Fruit salad. Cantaloupe and blue-berries, honeydew, watermelon."

All-time favorite dessert?

"Not chocolate cake because that's too chocolatey.

Thinking...I'm at home, I'm opening the fridge and I'm wishing something was there. What would that thing be? Hmmm... dessert...homemade apple pie!"

13:

Managing Stress

Life is stressful to begin with, and we tend to make our lives more stressful than they need to be. It's important not to just manage your own stress, as Chief Executive Mom, but to be attuned to your family and come up with ways to help everyone manage their stress and tough emotions. In case you haven't noticed, kids have it hard as well, especially these days. So don't just save stress for you and your husband. Chances are your kids have got a lot on their minds too.

To help manage stress in our household, our family practices meditation as a mental exercise. Some folks practice for spiritual reasons, some folks pray. I prefer to use this tactic for brain exercise. One of my favorite books to help with meditation practice is by Sharon Salzberg, called *Real Happiness: The Power of Meditation*. It gives instructions on different ways to meditate, lists all of the health benefits, and shares links to some guided meditations.

With our rate of going a mile a minute, it is so important to slow down and gain control of our brains and bodies, even if it's just for a short period of time. If you have never meditated before, I would suggest starting with ten minutes at a time. On really stressful days or on days that I'm feeling a like my thoughts are less positive, I do twenty minutes.

Meditation reminds me how small we are and how short our time is. It allows me to compartmentalize all of what is happening around me and focus. Focus on what? It varies. Sometimes it's my breath (because it's the only thing I have with me): sometimes it's a spot on the wall, sometimes it's vivid imagery. The important thing is that when I hold the object of focus in my sights, it's the only thing I hold until I choose to let it go. In my experience, being in control of what you hold onto and let go of is crucial in managing stressful situations.

Being Mom/ Wife/ Homemaker, a.k.a Chief Executive Mom, is the most stressful and rewarding job we will ever have. Above all, our mental health is the most important element to take care of. Reconnecting with yourself, finding your happiness and building your team are all steps that lead to making you mentally stronger. But let's be real—you will have days where everything will fall apart, there will be tears, sometimes from the kids and sometimes from you. The best advice I can give on managing your stress is to remember that every moment eventually passes. It's OK to take a timeout and it's important for the kids to understand that timeouts are not a bad thing, they are simply a time to relax, reflect and regain our thoughts so that we can resume our day on our own terms. Timeout can be that peaceful quiet from meditation or it can be listening to your favorite song.

Timeout also allows us to learn about our own boundaries and when we need the quiet time so that we can model this for the rest of the family, thereby helping them understand when they've been overstimulated and need quiet time as well.

Another way to alleviate stress is to celebrate all failures and coach our team into trusting that failure is just an opportunity for us to stand up again and succeed. In one of my favorite meditations, stress is acknowledged as our body's natural response to growth. If we keep that in mind, in our most stressful times we can respond accordingly and be grateful that we all get to grow and learn together as a team.

⇆ Feedback From The Team

Here's what one of my children said when I asked them, What do you when you get stressed out?

"I think about why I'm stressed out and then I get stressed out more and then I just sit for a while and try to work on the thing I'm stressed out on. Sometimes I just give up—well not give up but take a break on it for a long time. Just taking a break on not thinking about it and then I try to forget that it happened for like ten minutes. Because when I leave my stress and I come back to it, it's easier than before and it doesn't seem so bad."

Conclusion

Looking back on all that we've covered in this book, remember that above all, your version of self-care and cultivating your relationship with your team is most important. In fact, I would remind you that in the span of the universe, no matter your religious beliefs, our time here, alive and now, is so limited. When I think about every interaction I have with my husband and my kids, I want to make them all count.

That doesn't mean that life is good and clean and happy all the time. But pick your battles. If I'm going to get stressed out and get on my kids' case, I'm going to be as mindful as I can about how that interaction should go.

One of my favorite quotes is by Mark Twain: "I've lived through some terrible things in my life, some of which actually happened." It's comical how often I've said that to myself over the years. Did the loved one making a mess actually do anything to me? No. Is the house being messy actually going to make me go crazy? No. It really takes a lot to stop myself from reacting sometimes. And yes, I do have to go back sometimes and apologize for reacting instead of responding because I am only human.

There is just so much pressure to do right all the time, and I wrote this book as a way of helping you let go of as much of that pressure as you can. I know I've improved my quality of life and that of my family drastically by shifting my mindset and being thoughtful about how I turned my family into a team.

I cannot emphasize enough that it's all about mindset. Are you a disgruntled housewife or an empowered homemaker? Are you a dictator or a leader? Are you a complainer or a problem solver? Do you let mainstream society determine how and what you teach your family? Think. Really think. I can give you all the tips you desire to make your home cleaner, quicker but the underlying mess will never resolve if you don't shift your mindset.

From this day forward, you're not just "Mom." You're definitely not, "Mom, have you seen my ...?" and you're not "So and so's Mom." You are YOU. And what YOU do currently is run the tightest household on the block. You're Chief Executive Mom. Not only that—you're the baddest Chief Executive Mom around. You run Your Household, Inc. like the best Fortune 500 company out there. And best of all, you've got a super-charged up team, engaged, eager to help, and loving you like crazy.

This might be the end of our time together, but this is really the beginning for you. You will train, you will coach, and you will lead. You will show them that you can still be happy when the house—and life—is imperfect. You will show your family that relationships and communication matter more than material things. You will teach your children how to live a fulfilling life on purpose and with purpose. And when all is said and done, you will be their greatest mentor and teammate. Now it's time, Momma. It's time to clock in.

If you are ready to finally let go of control and take your place as the Chief Executive Mom, or to find out more about me and what I do, please visit: www.JenniferLLopez.com

Appendix A:
Assistant Pro 3-Step Methodology

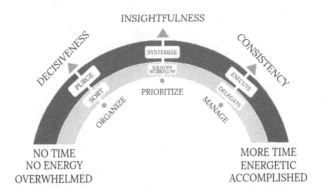

3 STEP METHODOLOGY

INSIGHTFULNESS

DECISIVENESS

CONSISTENCY

SYSTEMIZE

IDENTIFY WORKFLOW

PURGE

EXECUTE

SORT

DELEGATE

PRIORITIZE

ORGANIZE

MANAGE

NO TIME
NO ENERGY
OVERWHELMED

MORE TIME
ENERGETIC
ACCOMPLISHED

"HAPPINESS IS NOT SOMETHING READY MADE. IT COMES
FROM YOUR OWN ACTIONS." - DALAI LAMA

Appendix B:
Battle of the Bedrooms

When I created *Battle of the Bedrooms*, we had been having a particularly nightmarish few months of keeping up with the kids' bedrooms. The words that usually worked, just didn't. Little by little the mess started to spread like cancer.

Before I knew it, the sea of Lego pieces and laundry had taken over the bedrooms. Knowing that the old "no friends over in a messy room" wasn't working, I knew I needed a new game to motivate us all. And so it was created: *Battle of the Bedrooms*!

What you'll need:

- 4 players (or 4 players +; in our case, Nora swapped teams throughout)
- Dice
- 1 penny
- 1 dime (if you have an automatic vacuum)
- 2 messy bedrooms

How to play:

1. Each of the 2 bedrooms is identified as "Heads" or "Tails."

2. Players sit in a circle to start. Each player takes turns rolling the die, go clockwise.

3. The first player to roll an even number sits out. The second player to roll an even number joins them. They are Team 1 while the remaining players are Team 2.

4. The first Team 1 member then flips the penny to determine which room is theirs to start. If the penny lands with "Heads" up then the room is "Heads." If the penny lands with "Tails" up, then the room is identified as "Tails."

5. Once the room is determined, one member of the second team flips the dime. If the dime lands on "Heads," they get to run the robot vacuum first. If it's "Tails", Team 2 gets the vacuum. (Note: this is only done in Round 1). (Once the vacuum is done in bonus room, the second room may use it.)

6. Both teams will now gather exactly in between both rooms. They must join hands in the middle until the Grand Time Master (me) counts down from three.

7. As the teams begin, the five-minute timer starts.

8. The teams will be judged on three categories to determine the winner:

9. Insides (in drawers/closets)

10. Outsides (general room tidiness)

11. Shine (the wipe down)

12. When the five-minute timer goes off, the teams must reconvene to the initial circle where they will roll the die again to determine Round 2 teams and assigned rooms.

13. The object of the game is to have an organized, clean, disinfected room.

Perks:

A. By switching teammates every round, the family finds ways to work well together with no unfair advantages (I was on everyone's team at least once.)

B. By flipping a coin for your work room every round, no player shows favor to any one room. The winning team is the team with the winning room (no matter how well the team in the previous round cleaned).

C. The beauty of *Battle of the Bedrooms* is if you started off with a cleaner room, your chances may be better to win. It encourages everyone to keep the rooms in a decent condition in case a battle arises.

D. Just because it's someone else's dirty laundry doesn't mean you can't help them out by bringing it to the laundry room. Very quickly, the mentality went from "That's *her stuff*" to "Hurry! Give it to me and I'll put it away!"

Prize:

Our kids love the ice cream place around the block probably more than oxygen. The players from the winning team each get a color counter chip. When a player retrieves six chips, they get a trip to their favorite ice cream shop. Players only surrender their chips on the day of said ice cream trip.

Appendix C:

Budget Binder Resources

Chief Executive Mom

Your Household Inc.

Profit & Loss Statement

Month: _____

	Projected	Cleared
Income		
Income 1		
Income 2		
Additional Income		
Gifts		
Total Income		
Expenses		
Mortgage/Rent		
Water		
Electricity		
Gas		

	Projected	Cleared
Home Phone/Cable		
Cell Phone		
Car Payment		
Car Payment		
Car Insurance		
Tolls		
Groceries		
General Maintenance		
Lawn Care		
Housekeeping/Supplies		
Entertainment		
Memberships		
Credit Cards		
Total Expenses		
Profit / (Loss)		
Income - Expenses		

Month	Checking Start	Checking End	Savings Start	Savings End
January				
February				
March				
April				
May				
June				
July				
August				
September				
October				
November				
December				

About the Author

Jennifer Lopez is the owner and founder of Assistant Pro, a rapidly growing concierge staffing agency committed to assisting middle class families with everyday repetitive tasks. A natural leader, she found success in management early before diving headfirst into a job with long hours, little gratitude, and zero pay: homemaking & homeschooling. With four kids, two dogs, and busy husband, Jennifer quickly saw what "in over your head" actually means. Eager to regroup quickly, she tried a different approach to running her household. Instead of stressing herself out constantly telling her family what to do, she drew from her early success in the workplace and started running her home the way she ran her stores. The pivot paid off. By empowering her family to take part of, and ownership in, the decision-making process, she discovered that the home had as much to gain from her expertise in task & team management as the workplace.

Chief Executive Mom is the product of this discovery.

Notes

CPSIA information can be obtained
at www.ICGtesting.com
Printed in the USA
BVHW070958150719
553472BV00004B/231/P